BACKPACKER®

Trailside
Recipes

Simple and Tasty Backcountry Fare

Edited by Molly Absolon

FALCONGUIDES

GUILFORD, CONNECTICUT
HELENA, MONTANA

AN IMPRINT OF GLOBE PEQUOT PRESS

FALCONGUIDES®

Copyright © 2012 by Morris Book Publishing, LLC

Backpacker is a registered trademark of Cruz Bay Publishing, Inc.
FalconGuides is an imprint of Globe Pequot Press.
Falcon, FalconGuides, and Outfit Your Mind are registered trademarks of Morris
Book Publishing, LLC.

Photos: Justin Bailie, unless otherwise credited
Text design: Sheryl P. Kober
Page layout: Justin Marciano
Project editor: Julie Marsh

Library of Congress Cataloging-in-Publication Data is available on file.

ISBN 978-0-7627-7297-1

Printed in China

10 9 8 7 6 5 4 3 2 1

Contents

Chapter Four: Desserts

Chapter Five: Beverages

Introduction

What do you eat on your backpacking trips? Are you one of those people who down an energy bar for dinner and call it good? Do you consider boiling water for instant oatmeal the height of your culinary expertise? Or are you spending most of your backcountry trip dreaming of the food you'll consume when you get back to town?

Maybe it's time for a culinary epiphany. Backcountry cooking doesn't have to be extravagant or time-consuming to be nutritious and tasty, but often it takes a nudge to get you out of your old habits to try something new. This book is your nudge.

For years each issue of *Backpacker* magazine has featured recipes designed specifically for campsite cooking. These recipes range widely from hearty cheesy pasta to Asian-inspired curries to individual-pan pizzas, and all share a few common traits: The meals are simple, easy to pack and prepare, and they can be cooked on a single-burner stove or campfire.

Now we've brought together more than one hundred of our all-time favorite recipes and compiled them into a lightweight, packable book so you can slip your menu inspiration into a pocket. No longer do you have to search *Backpacker*'s website or flip through back issues of the magazine looking for recipe ideas for your next backcountry trip. Just grab your cookbook and head to the store. Next thing you know, you'll be enjoying green Thai curry rather than instant ramen noodles after a long day on the trail.

We've grouped the recipes under the categories breakfast, lunch, dinner, desserts, and beverages. Each recipe includes a list of ingredients, followed by at-home tips to make meal preparation easier in camp. Then we give you detailed cooking instructions, hints for tasty variations, and occasionally reader suggestions that enhance the recipe.

So take a moment to flip through these pages, pick out some enticing recipes, gather up your ingredients, and head to the mountains armed with everything you need to change your backcountry menu from bland and boring to gourmet.

Chapter One

Breakfast

You've heard it countless times: Breakfast is the most important meal of the day. You may argue this in town, but in the backcountry there is little room for debate. A hearty breakfast gets you going in the morning, fuels you down the trail, and helps you stay warm in inclement weather. So load up on the calories—it's one of the few times you can justify eating with abandon.

EGG RECIPES

Omelet in a Bag

Mix it, bag it, and forget about it until breakfast time. Then what do you get? An instant yummy omelet.

2 eggs
2 tablespoons grated cheese
2 tablespoons salsa
2 tablespoons chopped ham
Pinch of salt and pepper
1 tablespoon cooking oil

At home: Pour lightly beaten eggs into a ziplock bag. Add the rest of the ingredients, plus anything else that sounds good. Double-bag the mixture to prevent a "sleeping bag-and-headlamp omelet."

In camp: Either pour the eggs out of the bag into a lightly oiled pan and fry, or bring a pot of water to a boil and drop the bag directly into the pot. Cook 5 to 7 minutes, until the eggs pull away from the sides of the bag.

(serves 1)

Packing Tip

You don't have to go with powdered eggs in the back-country. Try prepackaged Egg Beaters or, better yet, crack fresh eggs into a plastic container with a leakproof top. You can also double-bag liquid eggs in ziplock bags, but be careful to seal the package carefully to prevent leaking. You might want to freeze the eggs to make them easier to pack—they'll thaw as you hike, so make sure the container is leakproof. Plastic egg containers are also available at outdoor stores. (See sidebar on page 6 for details on how long eggs will keep in the outdoors.)

Herb-Scrambled Eggs

Enjoy a taste of Provence for breakfast, or perhaps you are looking for a Southwestern flair? Simply change up the herbs in this dish to shift its flavor.

2 eggs
$1/2$ cup jerky, ripped into small pieces
Dried parsley, marjoram, basil, and thyme to taste
1 English muffin or pita
1 tablespoon cooking oil

At home: Mix desired spices in a ziplock bag. Pack oil in leak-proof container.

In camp: Beat eggs in a bowl; add jerky and spices. Scramble mixture in a lightly oiled pan over medium heat. Spoon into pita or English muffin and enjoy!

(serves 1)

Variation: For a Southwestern flavor, substitute a pinch of chili powder or cumin for the herbs and serve with salsa.

Sierra Scrambled Eggs

Adding buttermilk to your eggs makes them creamy and gives you an added nutritional boost to fuel you through the day.

    5 eggs
    1/4 teaspoon pepper
    2 tablespoons dried bell pepper
    1 tablespoon dried onion
    4 teaspoons powdered buttermilk
    1 teaspoon garlic powder
    1 tablespoon oil

At home: Pack all the dry ingredients in a ziplock bag; transfer oil to a leakproof container.

In camp: Beat eggs in a bowl; add dry ingredients. Oil pan, then scramble egg mixture.

(serves 2)

Fresh Foods That Last Longer

Worried about foods spoiling on your camping trip? Here are a few tips to help you choose items that will stay fresh even in the summer.

Chocolate: Semisweet chocolate (it lacks meltable milk solids) and carob resist melting. Store in the center of your pack.

Cheese: Waxed or hard cheeses, such as cheddar, Colby, and Swiss, can last a week (several days longer than soft ones). Cheese may get oily in warm temperatures and not be all that palatable for lunchtime snacking, but it is still fine for cooking.

Eggs: Raw whole eggs, Egg Beaters, and eggs cracked and carried in a plastic container will keep about a week. Make sure to store them in a shady spot during the day.

Fruit: Apples and oranges stay good for a week plus. For soft fruit, like pears, buy them hard and let ripen on the trail.

Veggies: Storing vegetables in paper bags stalls spoilage for up to a week. Carrots, potatoes, and onions keep three weeks.

Butter: Butter lasts a week, or use ghee or margarine for a three-week lifespan.

Meats: Hard salami, jerky, and smoked meats stay good for weeks.

Huevos Revueltos con Papas

The real breakfast of champions? Potassium-rich potatoes, eggs, and zesty jalapeños.

3 ounces powdered eggs (such as Backpacker's
   Pantry)
1 tablespoon powdered milk
³/₄ cup plus 1¹/₂ tablespoons water
2–3 tablespoons olive or canola oil
2–3 medium-size potatoes
2–3 jalapeños, diced
1 small onion, chopped
¹/₂ teaspoon adobo seasoning
¹/₂ teaspoon chipotle seasoning
Salt and pepper to taste
Tortillas (optional)

At home: Combine powdered eggs and powdered milk in a ziplock bag.

In camp: Add water to powdered eggs/milk mixture; set aside. Coat skillet with oil. Chop potatoes and cook for 5 minutes. Add jalapeños and onion to skillet; sprinkle with adobo, chipotle, salt, and pepper. Cook for 10 minutes, or until potatoes are browned. Add eggs; stir and cook until set. For extra spice, garnish with additional chipotle or adobo seasoning. Eat as is or wrap in tortillas.

(serves 4–5)

Sun-Dried Tomato and Herb Frittata

Frittatas slip right out of the pan, making cleanup easy. Save any leftovers for a savory, filling lunch.

    1 tablespoon olive oil
    1/2 cup chopped sun-dried tomatoes
    1 teaspoon dried oregano
    1 teaspoon dried basil
    4 eggs (or 1 cup liquid egg substitute or the
        powdered equivalent of 4 eggs)
    2 tablespoons grated Parmesan or mozzarella
        cheese

In camp: Heat oil in a skillet over medium heat. Sauté sun-dried tomatoes until well coated (about 1 minute). Reduce heat to low. Mix oregano and basil with eggs and pour into skillet over tomatoes. Cover and cook 5 to 7 minutes, or until the mixture is almost set on top. Flip carefully; cook for 1 or 2 more minutes. Slide onto a plate, cut in half, and top with cheese.

(serves 2)

Jon's Favorite Trailside Pancakes

This basic pancake recipe is designed to let you mix things up according to what's in season, on sale, or in your cupboard.

50/50 blend of buttermilk pancake mix (Krusteaz preferred) and buckwheat pancake mix (Aunt Jemima preferred)

Eggs—critical for maximum fluffiness—or Egg Beaters (check pancake mix packages to determine how many)

Water as specified on package instructions

1 teaspoon vanilla

1 tablespoon cooking oil

Suggested additions as available

Nuts such as pecans, crumbled

Dark chocolate chips, 10 or fewer per 6-inch cake

Seasonal fruit (blueberries, raspberries, etc.)

Maple syrup or honey

In camp: Mix all the ingredients from mix through oil. Fold in additions one at a time—nuts, chips, then fruit—being careful not to mash the berries. Make one extra-large pancake at a time in a medium skillet, using very hot (but not smoking) oil for extra-crispy edges. Bring a real spatula, and use a heat diffuser if you have a stove with a very tightly focused flame that burns the middle of the cake while leaving the outside raw. Serve with warmed real maple syrup or honey.

Lemony Maple-Blueberry Syrup

Spice up your pancakes, oatmeal, French toast, breads, or cakes with this fun variation on classic maple syrup.

$1/2$ lemon (juice and rind)
1 tablespoon butter
$1/2$ pint fresh blueberries (substitutes: any other berry, or a soft fruit such as peach, pear, or plum)
$1/2$ cup real maple syrup
1 tablespoon brown sugar

At home: Pack syrup in a leakproof bottle; pack sugar in a ziplock bag.

In camp: Using a sharp knife, gently peel the yellow part of the lemon rind. Avoid cutting too deeply into the white part of the skin (it's bitter). Finely chop the yellow peel and set aside. Squeeze remaining lemon over a bowl to extract juice. In a skillet, melt the butter over low heat, then add the blueberries. Mash some of the blueberries with a fork, then add the remaining ingredients, including the lemon rind and juice. Simmer over low heat for about 5 minutes until the mixture starts to thicken.

(makes 1 cup)

Downeast Blueberry Pancakes

When the berries are ripe for picking, no true backcountry chef leaves blueberry pancakes off the menu.

2 cups all-purpose flour
2 teaspoons baking powder
$1/3$ cup powdered milk
$1/2$ teaspoon salt
2 cups water
3 tablespoons cooking oil
$1/3$ cup blueberries

At home: Combine the first four ingredients in a ziplock bag.

In camp: Add water and 2 tablespoons oil to flour mixture and knead the bag until combined; stir in blueberries. Heat remaining oil in a pan until it sizzles. Drop 4-inch circles of batter into the pan and cook 2 minutes, or until bubbles form on top. Flip and cook 1 minute more, or until pancakes are golden brown.

(serves 4)

Chef's Secret
To substitute dried blueberries for fresh, soak berries in $1/2$ cup water for 5 minutes. Make batter using $1^1/2$ cups water, then add the berries and water.

Blueberry-Hazelnut Rice Flour Pancakes

This gluten-free variation on the traditional recipe serves up superlight cakes.

- 1¼ cups rice flour
- 2 tablespoons sugar
- 2 teaspoons baking powder
- ½ teaspoon salt
- ¼ cup chopped hazelnuts
- ¼ cup fresh or dried blueberries
- 1¼ cups water
- 1–2 tablespoons canola oil

At home: Combine flour, sugar, baking powder, salt, and hazelnuts (plus blueberries, if you're using dried) in a large ziplock bag.

In camp: Combine dry ingredients with water and oil (plus blueberries, if you're using fresh) in a medium-size bowl. Heat a lightly greased skillet over medium flame. Spoon 3 tablespoons of batter onto skillet; cook 2 to 3 minutes per side until browned.

(serves 3)

Peanut Butter and Jelly Pancakes

Pancakes don't stick to your ribs for long, unless you add peanut butter.

- 1¼ cups all-purpose flour
- 2 tablespoons sugar
- 2 teaspoons baking powder
- ½ teaspoon salt
- 1¼ cups water
- ¼ cup peanut butter
- 1–2 tablespoons cooking oil
- ½ cup jelly, jam, or preserves, any flavor

At home: Combine first four ingredients in a ziplock bag.

In camp: In a medium size bowl, combine dry ingredients with water and mix thoroughly. Fold in peanut butter. Heat and lightly grease a skillet with cooking oil. Pour 3 tablespoons of batter onto skillet for each pancake. Cook on both sides until browned, 2 to 3 minutes each side. Serve with jam, jelly, or preserves.

(serves 3)

Chef's Secret

Pack a supply of single-serving jelly packets to avoid carrying a container of jelly. Allow for 3 to 4 packets per serving.

Shannon's Choco-Banana French Toast

This gooey concoction will leave you decadently stuffed. It's kind of elaborate, but perfect for car camping or yurt trips.

3 large eggs (or Egg Beaters' equivalent)
$1/2$ cup milk
2 tablespoons plain yogurt (optional)
$1/2$ teaspoon ground cinnamon
2 tablespoons vanilla
2 tablespoons butter
1 cup Nutella
16 $1/2$-inch slices of French bread
2 large bananas, sliced

In camp: Stir eggs, milk, yogurt, cinnamon, and vanilla until smooth. Set aside. Heat some butter in a large nonstick skillet/griddle/cast-iron pan over medium heat. Spread Nutella on one side of each slice of French bread. Top half of the bread slices with several banana slices. Place the remaining bread slices Nutella-side down on top of the bananas. Dip each sandwich carefully in the egg mixture (tongs help) and turn to coat, making sure to keep the sandwich intact. Place the sandwiches on the hot skillet and cook until golden brown. Turn gently, and cook on the other side until golden brown. Serve the Nutella French toast immediately, garnished with fresh berries and a drizzle of pure maple syrup.

(makes 8 sandwiches)

Vanilla-Walnut Crepes

Sweet crepes are often served as a dessert in France, but in the mountains? Why not eat them for breakfast?

1 cup all-purpose flour
1/4 cup instant French vanilla cappuccino or hot
    chocolate mix (such as Wild Harvest)
2 teaspoons baking powder
1/2 teaspoon salt
1 1/3 cups water
1–2 tablespoons cooking oil
3/4 cup chopped walnuts
2 cups dried cranberries and/or cherries
1/4 cup powdered sugar

At home: Combine first four ingredients in a ziplock bag.

In camp: In a medium-size bowl, mix dry ingredients with water until smooth. Heat and lightly grease a skillet with cooking oil. Spoon 3 tablespoons of batter onto skillet; swirl skillet until the batter spreads out thin. Cook 1 to 2 minutes per side until browned. Remove from the pan. Fill with walnuts and sliced fruit, roll up and sprinkle with powdered sugar.

(serves 3)

Chef's Secret

Use watered-down pancake batter to make crepes in camp. Pancake mix is sweeter than crepe mix, which makes it better for dessert crepes than meal crepes.

No-Frills Crepes

Crepes can be made with either sweet or savory batter, and served with just about anything: sugar, fruit, cheese, meat. Your only limitation is your imagination.

3 large eggs

1 1/3 cups whole milk

3/4 cup unbleached, all-purpose flour

3/4 teaspoon salt

5 tablespoons unsalted butter, melted

At home: Mix all the ingredients together and blend until smooth. Pour 1/4 cup at a time into a buttered 8-inch skillet over medium heat. When the edges are noticeably crispy, flip the crepe. Lift the edge with a spatula, then flip with your hands to avoid tearing. Cook until golden brown. Let the crepes cool, then stack them, separated with pieces of wax paper, and put into a large ziplock bag. Store flat like a stack of tortillas in the fridge. Crepes last up to three days on the trail.

(serves 3)

HEARTY POTATO BREAKFASTS

Sausage and Potato Breakfast

A hearty breakfast like this one hits the spot on cold, wet mornings in the mountains.

2 tablespoons powdered scrambled egg mix

Enough powdered milk to make the milk required
for potatoes

1 3.5-ounce packet instant cheesy mashed potatoes
1/2 cup chopped cooked Italian sausage
1/2 teaspoon garlic powder
1 tablespoon butter

In camp: Mix powdered eggs, powdered milk, and potato flakes. Add boiling water (use the amount specified on potato package directions). Stir in sausage, garlic powder, and butter. Eat!

(serves 3–4)

Bacon and Cheese Breakfast Taters

This recipe is a little more involved than pouring hot water into oatmeal—but thanks to extra-convenient ingredients, not much.

1 2-ounce Jack Link's Jack Pack! (combo of cheese sticks, beef sticks, and pretzels)
1 3-ounce pouch bacon bits
Small green onion, chopped
1 tablespoon oil
1 3.5-ounce packet instant cheesy mashed potatoes (recommend Hungry Jack Easy Mash'd Mashed Potatoes, Cheesy Homestyle)
1 tablespoon grated Parmesan cheese (use one of the packets from your last pizza delivery)
2 teaspoons Kraft Macaroni & Cheese Topping

In camp: Dice the Jack Pack cheese sticks. Slice beef sticks into 1/4-inch-thick rings. Sauté beef with bacon bits and chopped onion in oil until barely tender. Add 2 cups water, cover, and bring to a boil (now's a good time to eat those pretzels that came in the Jack Pack!). Remove from heat and stir in mashed potato mix and Parmesan cheese. Potatoes will thicken quickly—smooth out any lumps with a spoon or spatula. Sprinkle with cheese topping and diced cheese. Enjoy!

(serves 2)

HOT CEREALS

Cheesy Grits

The secret to grits lies in how well they complement any and all toppings. Whether you add sweet sundries (like bananas with brown sugar), salty and savory tidbits (ham, cheese, bacon, beans), or spicy foods (a handful of jalapeños), the ground cornmeal's mild flavor and amazing velvety texture enhance all accoutrements.

Pinch of salt

1 cup water

3 tablespoons regular grits

Your choice of toppings (see sidebar)

In camp: Add a pinch of salt to the water, bring it to a boil, and then add the grits. Cover the pot and turn the heat to low, stirring the grits regularly to make them soft and silky smooth. Keep cooking until the desired softness is reached. Different grits cook at different rates. Quick-cooking varieties usually take 8 to 10 minutes, while regular grits take about 20 minutes. To finish off your breakfast, add your desired toppings.

(serves 1)

Toppings and Mix-ins

» Handful of diced cheese cubes (any cheese works, but American melts easily) and some slices of summer sausages, or cheese and freeze-dried broccoli for a veggie alternative (toss the dried broccoli in with the grits to cook)
» Apple and peanut butter—fantastic!
» Powdered milk (no need to reconstitute the milk first; just add slightly more water to the pot if needed) plus garlic and onion powder
» A handful of gorp
» Plain ol' delicious butter and salt

Ramps 'n' Grits

Add garlicky zing to classic southern Appalachian grits.

2 ramps (wild leeks), white part only, minced, or substitute 1 clove garlic, minced, plus 3 green onions, white part only, chopped
1 teaspoon vegetable oil
2 cups water
4 1-ounce packets instant grits, plain or bacon
Black pepper to taste

In camp: Fry ramps (or garlic/green onions) in oil until fragrant. Add water and bring to a boil. Whisk in grits and season with pepper.

(serves 4)

Wild Leeks

Wild leeks (*Allium tricoccum*), or ramps, grow in sandy, moist soils from the Southeast to southern Canada. Medical studies show that this pungent relative of onions and garlic lowers blood pressure, alleviates hay fever and bladder problems, and works as an antiseptic. Look for ramps in the early spring before the trees leaf out. Their bright green, smooth, oval-shaped leaves stand out from the brown leaves of the forest floor. Dig up the bulbs and smell. You'll know if you have the right plant.

Trail Brecky

If you think oatmeal is boring and tasteless, think again. This recipe will change your mind. Plus everybody knows oats are good for our hearts.

3 cups water or milk (use powdered milk)
1 cup rolled oats
Handful of dried cranberries
Handful of sunflower seeds
1 teaspoon ground cinnamon
2 tablespoons butter
2 tablespoons brown sugar or beet syrup

In camp: Place water and oats in a pot and bring to a boil. Reduce heat to a simmer and cook until soft and creamy. Add the rest of the ingredients, stir, and enjoy.

(serves 2–3)

Breakfast Pan-Fried Noodles

Tired of the same old breakfast routines? What about fried noodles for a change?

1 pound buckwheat or whole-wheat spaghetti

2 tablespoons sesame oil

1 onion, minced

1 carrot, grated

3 cloves garlic, minced

2 tablespoons tamari soy sauce

1/2 cup finely chopped cashews

6 eggs

1 teaspoon salt

1/2 teaspoon crushed red pepper flakes

At home: Cook spaghetti according to package directions and drain. Heat oil in a Dutch oven over medium heat. Add onion, carrot, and garlic and cook for 5 minutes. Add spaghetti and cook 5 more minutes, stirring, until pasta is browned. Stir in soy sauce and cashews; cook 1 minute. Beat eggs. Add eggs, salt, and red pepper flakes; cook 5 minutes, or until eggs are set. Spread mixture on dehydrator trays; dehydrate 4 hours on 145ºF. Pack in ziplock bags.

In camp: Place noodles in a pot. Pour water in until food is just covered. Heat to a boil, stir, and enjoy.

(serves 4)

Cheesy Bagel

The ultimate breakfast sandwich: fast, filling, and full of calories to fuel your day.

1 bagel
Squeeze butter
2 slices precooked bacon
Onion slices to taste
Extra-sharp cheddar cheese to taste
Hot sauce (optional)

In camp: Cut bagel in half. Squeeze some butter into a frying pan and fry one half, sliced-side down, until browned (flip it once). Repeat with the other half. While bagel is cooking, slice bacon strips in half. Also slice onion and cheese. When bagel is toated, top with bacon, cheese, and onion. Continue cooking until cheese melts and the whole thing begins to stick together. Place one bagel half on top of the cheesy concoction and press down gently; the filling should stick to the bagel. Remove from pan, add desired amount of hot sauce, and top with the other bagel half to finish the sandwich.

(serves 1)

Chapter Two

Lunch

On most backcountry trips, lunch begins with the completion of breakfast and ends with the start of dinner. Typically we snack throughout the day—a handful of gorp, an energy bar or two—to keep our energy up on the trail. This chapter provides ideas for immediate on-the-trail gratification, plus suggestions for more elaborate fare—because sometimes it's nice to enjoy a leisurely meal that involves a little preparation. Finally, some fast, easy twists on typical sandwiches and trail food add variety and flavor to your hikes.

PACKABLE, PORTABLE WRAPS

Olympic Wrap

The lunch choice of champions . . . or at least it should be.

> 1 tube tomato paste
> 1 or 2 whole-wheat tortillas
> Manchego cheese (Hard cheeses are best because
>   they last longer. Plus, they're delicious.)
> Turkey pepperoni

On the trail: Squeeze tomato paste onto a tortilla. Slice cheese and layer with pepperoni on the tortilla, then wrap and eat. Repeat as necessary.

(serves 1)

BCT Roll-Up

Backcountry BLT: bacon, cheese, and tomatoes.

2 packets mayonnaise
2 flour tortillas
2 tablespoons bacon bits
5 sun-dried tomatoes (¹/₂ ounce), minced
2 ounces cheddar cheese sticks

On the trail: Squeeze one mayo packet onto a tortilla. Sprinkle some bacon and tomato pieces on top. Top with one cheese stick. Wrap and eat. Repeat with remaining ingredients.

(serves 2)

Beef Veggie Wraps

A bit of Tex-Mex spice adds to this midday snack.

3 tablespoons dried ground beef
¹/₄ cup plus 2 tablespoons instant hash browns
¹/₄ cup thinly sliced dried carrots
¹/₄ cup thinly sliced sun-dried tomatoes
1 tablespoon dried onions
4 flour tortillas
¹/₂ cup salsa

At home: Pack all the dried ingredients in a ziplock bag.

In camp: Place dried ingredients in a bowl and add 1 cup plus 3 tablespoons boiling water. Mix, cover, and let stand for 10 minutes. Heat tortillas in a frying pan or pot lid. When meat and veggies have fully rehydrated, drain any excess water and mix in salsa. Spoon ½ cup of the mixture into each tortilla, fold, and eat.

(serves 2)

Tuna Salad Wraps with Sprouts

A simple tuna salad gets a nutritional punch with the addition of bean sprouts.

1 4.5 ounce pouch tuna
¼ cup mung sprouts
2 tablespoons mayonnaise and/or mustard
Garlic powder to taste
2 corn tortillas

In camp: In a bowl, mix tuna with mung sprouts, mayonnaise and/or mustard, and garlic powder. Wrap into a warm tortilla, roll up, and bite in.

(serves 1)

Banana Peanut Butter Roll-Up

Kids—and adults—will love this easy lunchtime treat.

1 tablespoon peanut butter
1 tablespoon Nutella or honey
1 flour tortilla
1 banana, sliced

On the trail: Spread peanut butter and/or Nutella and/or honey over a tortilla. Add banana and roll. Wrap entire roll in tinfoil to prevent it from unrolling or oozing in your pack if you're not going to eat it right away.

(serves 1)

CLASSIC SANDWICHES WITH A TWIST

Supreme Crusty Bread Sandwiches

This hot sandwich is perfect for those days where you're sticking close to camp with a fire still smoldering.

1 loaf crusty bread (French, sourdough, etc.)
Butter or olive oil
Swiss cheese*
Ham*
Mushrooms (canned is lovely)*

In camp: Lay the loaf of bread on a piece of tinfoil big enough to cover the entire loaf. Make slices in the bread without completely cutting through the loaf. Swipe a little butter or olive oil on the insides of every cut. Layer your toppings within every other cut. Run a little butter/oil across the top of the whole loaf (or don't; this is not an essential step). Wrap the tinfoil snugly around the overflowing loaf. Heat over campfire coals or in a frying pan over stove until the cheese is melted. Cut or tear into sandwich size pieces.

(makes 6–8 sandwiches)

*Replace with anything of your choosing.

Smoked Salmon Sliders

Sliders are greasy little burgers that are supposed to slide right down your throat. These sandwiches are little and they do slide right down, but not because they are greasy. They're just that good.

- 6 ounces smoked salmon
- 1 tablespoon chopped green onions
- 1 tablespoon chopped red onions
- 1 tablespoon capers
- 2 tablespoons minced fresh dill
- 1 tablespoon fresh lemon juice
- 1 teaspoon mustard
- 1 tablespoon olive oil
- 10 mini bagels

In camp: Shred salmon in a bowl and mix in other ingredients, except bagels. Split and toast bagels, make sandwiches with salmon mixture. Optional: Add cream cheese or cucumber.

(makes 10 sliders)

Spicy Chicken Salad Sandwiches

PB&J is for amateurs. This spiced-up sandwich is just what your taste buds need on the trail.

- 1 7-ounce pouch precooked chicken breast
- 1 8-ounce can corn
- 1/4 cup crumbled bacon
- 1/2 cup grated Parmesan cheese
- 1 1/2 teaspoons dried cilantro
- 1/4 teaspoon ground cumin
- 1/4 teaspoon garlic powder
- 1/8 teaspoon chili powder
- Salt and pepper to taste
- 4 1-ounce packets ranch dressing
- 2 ciabatta rolls, halved

At home: Drain corn and double-bag in ziplock bags. Place bacon pieces and Parmesan into two separate bags. Spoon spices into another ziplock bag; shake to combine.

In camp: Mix chicken, corn, bacon, and Parmesan in a bowl. Stir in spices and ranch dressing. Spread half the mixture on each roll.

(makes 2 sandwiches)

Chef's Secret

For a tasty alternative to Dijon mustard and cream cheese, try pesto sauce.

Cinnamon-Raisin PB Sandwiches

Okay, we just said PB&J is for amateurs, but not this version. Add a few secret ingredients and you have gourmet PB&J suitable for all ages.

- ¹/₂ cup peanut butter
- 2 tablespoons honey
- 1 teaspoon ground cinnamon
- 6–8 slices bread
- 4 tablespoons raisins

At home: In a bowl, mix together peanut butter, honey, and cinnamon. Spread peanut butter mixture over a slice of bread. Sprinkle approximately 1 tablespoon raisins evenly over peanut butter mixture and place another slice of bread on top to complete the sandwich. Repeat with remaining ingredients.

(makes 3–4 sandwiches)

Variations: Try different dried fruit and nut butters, like cranberries with cashew butter, or bananas with almond butter or even sunflower seed butter.

Californian Sandwiches

A summery vegetarian sandwich that is not only good for you, it tastes great too.

2 yellow squashes
4 ounces hummus
6–8 slices bread
Red cabbage, shredded (about 1/2 head)
2 avocados, peeled and thinly sliced
2 ounces alfalfa sprouts

At home: Thinly slice yellow squash. Spread slices onto a paper towel and sprinkle with salt. Set squash aside for about 15 minutes. Spread hummus on bread. Pat squash slices dry and place them on top of hummus. After squash, layer on red cabbage, avocado slices, and alfalfa sprouts. This sandwich is also good in a pita or wrap.

(makes 3–4 sandwiches)

Chef's Secret
Drier and denser breads are generally better for backcountry sandwiches. Try a crusty baguette, ciabatta bread, tortilla, or pita. If you slather fillings that have high moisture content onto soft, fluffy bread, you will have a soggy lunch.

Packing Tip

For some of us, it is hard to imagine a sandwich being complete without lettuce and tomato. But keep in mind those items have high water content (hence the sog factor). Instead consider vegetables such as fennel, spinach, or shredded cabbage. If you want toppings like tomato, pickles, or cucumber, pack them separately.

Turkey and Swiss Sandwich

We hear you: Who needs a recipe for a turkey and Swiss sandwich? Well, did it ever occur to you to add cream cheese? Try it.

1 teaspoon Dijon mustard
2 slices bread
Turkey, thinly sliced
Baby spinach, washed (optional)
2 slices Swiss cheese
1 teaspoon cream cheese

On the trail: Spread Dijon mustard on one slice of bread and top with turkey. Pat spinach dry and place on top of turkey along with slices of Swiss cheese. Spread cream cheese on the other slice of bread and close sandwich.

(makes 1 sandwich)

Avocado and Ham Sandwiches

Dijon mustard adds some tang—and sophistication, remember the Rolls Royce?—to this classic ham sandwich.

2 tablespoons butter, softened
1 tablespoon Dijon mustard
Pinch of black pepper
4–6 slices bread
Sliced ham
1 avocado, peeled and thinly sliced

On the trail: Mix together butter, Dijon, and black pepper. Spread on both slices of bread and layer with ham and avocado.

(makes 2–3 sandwiches)

MIDDLE EASTERN LUNCHES

Falafel with Tahini Sauce

Boost your on-trail protein intake with this tasty dish.

1 cup falafel mix
Vegetable oil (enough for frying)
2 tablespoons tahini (sesame paste)
2 cloves garlic, minced
2 tablespoons lemon juice
Salt to taste
2 large pita pockets, halved

In camp: Add ¾ cup water to falafel mix and mix thoroughly; let sit for 10 minutes. Shape falafel into small patties and fry in oil, on both sides, to desired crispiness. To make the sauce, combine remaining ingredients (except pita), and thin it with warm water to the consistency you want. Put falafel patties into pita pockets, spoon on sauce, and dig in

(serves 2)

Crunchy Tabbouleh

Tabbouleh's minty taste provides a welcome change from your regular backcountry flavors.

1 6-ounce box tabbouleh mix (including spice packet)
1 small cucumber
2 green onions
1 carrot
2 radishes
1/2 cup broccoli florets
4 sprigs parsley
2 tablespoons lemon juice (optional)
2 tablespoons olive oil
2 flour tortillas or pita pockets

At home: Combine bulgur from tabbouleh mix with contents of spice packet; pack in a ziplock bag.

In camp: At breakfast, chop the veggies and parsley, and combine all ingredients in a leakproof container with 1 cup cold, filtered water. By lunchtime, the bulgur will be rehydrated and the salad will be ready to devour. Serve with tortillas or pita pockets.

(serves 2)

SNACKS

Apple-Raisin "No Freeze" Oatmeal Bars

An easy, year-round homemade snack.

- 1 1/2 cups rolled oats, uncooked
- 1 1/3 cups all-purpose flour
- 2/3 cup light brown sugar
- 3/4 cup butter (softened)
- 1 large apple, chopped into pieces (about 1 1/2 cups)
- 1/2 cup raisins
- 1/2 cup shredded carrots (optional)
- 1/4 teaspoon ground cinnamon
- 1/8 teaspoon salt

At home: Preheat oven to 400°F. Mix together oats, flour, and brown sugar. Cut in butter until mix is crumbly. Add apple, raisins, carrots, cinnamon, and salt, mixing well. Pat mixture into a greased 9 x 9-inch pan, bake for 40 minutes, and cool in pan before cutting.

(makes 18 chewy, all-natural energy snacks)

Maple-Almond-Banana Trail Mix

A big step up from store-bought granola.

4 tablespoons unsalted butter, melted

1 cup pure maple syrup

2 cups almonds, salted or unsalted

3 cups rolled oats

1 cup (about 4 ounces) dried bananas, cut into $1/2$-inch pieces

$2/3$ cup (about 3 ounces) dried cranberries

At home: Preheat oven to 375°F. Combine butter, maple syrup, almonds, and oats in a large bowl. Spread mixture on a rimmed baking sheet doused in cooking spray or a little butter. Bake, stirring once and rotating sheet after 20 minutes, until golden, 35 to 40 minutes total. Let cool. Transfer to a large plastic bag and dump in dried bananas and cranberries. Shake. Throw, literally, in backpack.

(makes 8 cups)

DEHYDRATED SNACKS

Burger Jerky

Say good-bye to rock-hard, overpriced, gas-station jerky with this cheap and easy recipe.

1 pound 80 percent lean ground beef

$1/2$ teaspoon garlic powder

2 tablespoons tamari or soy sauce
1 tablespoon chili powder
1 tablespoon Worcestershire sauce

At home. Preheat oven to 150°F (or "warm" setting). Mix beef and spices well in a large bowl. Place half of the meat on a sheet of wax paper and roll it to ⅛-inch thickness with a rolling pin. Cut the beef into 1-by-6-inch strips with a knife or pizza cutter and place on ungreased cookie sheets. Repeat with the other half. Dry in oven 7 to 12 hours (until strips break when bent) on the middle rack, flipping strips and patting excess fat dry with a paper towel every 3 to 4 hours. Let cool completely before storing in a ziplock bag. **Note:** Jerky can also be dried in a dehydrator set to 150°F.

(makes 12–14 strips)

Dehydrating Food

Dehydrating your own food is one of simplest ways to upgrade your backcountry menu. You can pack healthier foods and reduce your pack weight significantly.

Here are a few tips for successful drying:

1. Buy a dehydrator. Yes, you can dry foods in a standard oven set to 150ºF (leave the door open slightly), but the circulating air in a commercial device does a faster and more even job. You also get trays specifically made for drying sauces, fruits, jerkies, and more. *Backpacker* is a big fan of the American Harvest Snackmaster; models range from $44 to $70; www.nesco.com.

2. Slice it thin. The first thing everyone makes is dried fruit and with good reason: Apple slices, pineapple rings, berries, and other sweet treats are a great way to carry dense calories and vitamins and spruce up bland gorp. Next up is usually jerky, which takes a few tries to master. (Hint: Buy the leanest meat or fish you can find.) For all of these foods, our advice is to cut your sections thinner than the books recommend. You might wind up a bit on the crunchier side with your apples (leave the skins on—yum), but the fruits and especially the jerkies will last longer in the field. They also dry faster and more evenly if you cut $1/4$-inch slices rather than the typical $3/8$-inch.

3. Spice it up. Tabasco on your salmon jerky is just a start. Next time you're in the spice aisle, check out the flavored salts and sugars. A tiny pinch of green chili sugar (yes, it exists!) sprinkled pre-drying on apples and pears will create the most popular snack in camp. Another favorite: smoked sea salt (popular in the Northwest) on dried peppers, tomatoes, and jerky. If the exotic spices are too much of a hassle, try something simple, like cayenne on your pineapple chunks, or brown sugar on your bananas.

Ted's Herky Jerky

Jerky is the classic backcountry snack.

- 1–1½ pounds flank steak
- ⅔ cup Worcestershire sauce
- ⅔ cup soy sauce
- 1 clove garlic, finely minced (or 1 teaspoon garlic powder)
- 2–3 teaspoons freshly ground black pepper
- 2 teaspoons onion powder
- 1 teaspoon liquid smoke
- 1 teaspoon cayenne pepper (or red pepper flakes)

At home. Trim excess fat from the steaks. Place meat and remaining ingredients in a gallon-size, ziplock freezer bag. Squish everything around for about 10 minutes, until all powder clumps are broken up and ingredients are well mixed. Place in refrigerator and marinate 3 to 6 hours. When you're done marinating, evenly distribute the strips of meat across the trays of your dehydrator. (Oven version: Put them directly on the racks, with a sheet of aluminum foil below to aid cleanup.) Set the dehydrator (or oven) to 150ºF and bake jerky for 7 to 10 hours, checking and patting dry every few hours. When jerky is fully dry, pack in a ziplock bag.

(makes enough for 2 jerky lovers for 2 to 3 days)

Packing Tip
Kept cool in an airtight ziplock bag, most jerky will last a month (the fattier the meat, the shorter the shelf life). Stash it in the freezer when at home to extend freshness.

Spicy Teriyaki Elk Jerky

Elk meat makes for a leaner, more tender—and always organic!—trail snack.

2 pounds elk (or venison) steaks or roast

$1/4$ tablespoon salt

$1 1/2$ teaspoons garlic powder

$1/4$ teaspoon black pepper

1 teaspoon ground ginger

3 tablespoons brown sugar

$1/4$ cup teriyaki sauce

$1/4$ cup tamari or soy sauce

At home: Starting with the steaks or roast slightly frozen (firm, but easy to slice), cut meat cross-grain (across the long fibers) into $1/8$-inch-thick strips. Combine remaining ingredients in a large bowl and add meat strips; cover and marinate in the refrigerator for 8 hours, stirring occasionally. Dry 7 to 12 hours in a dehydrator set to 140ºF (or until strips break when bent). Cool completely before storing in a ziplock bag. **Note:** Jerky can also be dried in an oven on the "warm" setting.

(makes 30 strips)

Fruit Leathers

Convenient and sweet without lots of added sugar.

1-pound bags of frozen berries, thawed and pureed
in a food processor (try raspberries, strawberries, blueberries, cranberries, or a mixture)
Alternative: applesauce in a jar (which now comes
in a variety of flavors such as watermelon,
berry, and peach mango)

At home: Spread the fruit puree thinly on a plastic dehydrator tray lined with wax or parchment paper. Place in the dehydrator for 8 to 16 hours, or until the fruit peels off in a thin sheet. Roll in wax paper and store in a ziplock bag.

Variations: Experiment with a dash of nutmeg or cinnamon, or for an exotic twist, try a bit of cayenne pepper to add some kick to your fruit leather.

Chapter Three

Dinner

By the time most of us roll into camp after a day on the trail, we're hungry. Very hungry. Most people's appetites go into overdrive when they are backpacking. Under these conditions, almost anything tastes good—the first night. But after several evenings eating the same thing, that bland dish may have you gagging. You also want to make sure your meals contain enough calories and nutrients to refill the tanks. So don't just settle for anything. It can be fun to make creative, flavorful—and easy—meals to savor in the evening. Consider it a reward to yourself for a job well done.

SOUTH OF THE BORDER FARE

Anaheim Skillet Quesadillas

Meet the comfort food of the Southwest.

1 small red onion
1 small red bell pepper
1 Anaheim chili pepper
2 tablespoons chopped flat-leaf parsley
2–3 tablespoons olive oil
4 flour tortillas
3/4 cup each shredded sharp cheddar and pepper
      jack cheese

½ teaspoon ground cumin
½ teaspoon chili powder
Chopped jalapeños
Orange Chili Salsa (see page 44) for garnish
(optional)

At home: Put shredded cheese in a ziplock bag.

In camp: Cut onion and peppers into thin 2-inch strips. Sauté them with parsley in olive oil until slightly tender (about 10 minutes); set aside. Place one tortilla in a skillet, adding slightly more olive oil if needed. Sprinkle with cheese, pepper mixture, cumin, and chili powder. When crispy, fold tortilla over and remove to a plate. Cut into wedges and top with jalapeños and salsa. Repeat for each quesadilla.

(serves 4)

Orange Chili Salsa

This light, fruity garnish is so good, you'll make it to eat at home.

1 red jalapeño
1 green jalapeño
1 tablespoon olive oil
1/4 cup slivered raw almonds
1 tablespoon chopped fresh cilantro or parsley
2 large navel oranges

In camp: Dice jalapeños and sauté in olive oil for about 8 minutes. Add almonds and chopped cilantro or parsley and sauté for 6 to 7 minutes more, or until almonds are lightly browned. Peel oranges and slice out segments, holding each orange over a bowl to catch the juice; cut segments into bite-size chunks. Squeeze juice from leftover orange membranes into bowl. Add chili mixture and toss.

(serves 4–5)

Chef's Secret
Tone down the heat by removing the jalapeños' seeds and membranes.

Easy, Cheesy Southwest Jambalaya

Tex-Mex meets Cajun with this simple, fast recipe. The trick: flavored rice packages to speed up the process and minimize the ingredients.

- 1 tablespoon chopped yellow, white, or green onion (or 1 teaspoon dried onion flakes)
- 2 tablespoons diced red bell pepper (or 1 teaspoon dried)
- 2 tablespoons diced celery (or 2 teaspoons dried)
- 1 2-ounce Jack Link's Jack Pack! (combo of cheese sticks, beef sticks, and pretzels)
- 1 4-ounce pouch precooked Southwest-flavored chicken breast (such as Bumblebee)
- 1 tablespoon olive oil
- 1 pouch Cajun Sides Red Beans & Rice (by Knorr-Lipton)

At home: Pack fresh veggies in paper bags. Tip: An easy way to carry green onions in your pack is in an old Wyler's or Crystal Light drink mix plastic canister.

In camp: Rehydrate veggies or chop fresh veggies. Open the Jack Pack, slice meat into ¼-inch chunks, and dice cheese. (The pretzels are your appetizer.) Chop chicken. Sauté vegetables and meat chunks in oil until tender. Add 2 cups of water, cover, and bring to a boil. Add chopped chicken and red beans and rice packet. Simmer, covered, for 8 minutes. Sprinkle with the diced cheese. Remove from heat and let stand, covered, for 3 minutes.

(serves 2–3)

Chicken Posole

Limed corn is the secret to this classic New Mexican comfort food. Flour tortillas and lime wedges are traditional accompaniments.

- ½ cup chopped onion
- 2 cloves garlic, minced
- 1 teaspoon dried oregano
- 1 teaspoon ground cumin
- 1 tablespoon olive oil
- 1 15-ounce can posole (limed corn) or hominy
- 1 4-ounce can chopped green chilies
- 1 7-ounce pouch precooked chicken breast
- 1 cube chicken bouillon
- 1 cup water
- 4 8-inch flour tortillas

At home: Place onion and garlic in a ziplock bag. Drain posole and chilies; combine in a separate bag.

In camp: Sauté onion, garlic, oregano, and cumin in oil until onion softens. Add remaining ingredients and bring to a boil, stirring to dissolve bouillon. Simmer 5 minutes, or until posole is heated through. Use tortillas to dip.

(serves 2)

Reader's Tip

Pack tortillas in your frying pan to preserve their shape and integrity.

Pepperoni Pizza in a Pan

Now you don't have to wait until you get back to town to enjoy a slice of pizza.

- 5-ounce block Asiago cheese (or another hard/ semihard cheese, such as Gouda, Monterey Jack, Parmigiana, or Reggiano)
- 1 6.5-ounce pouch baking mix (such as Bisquick or Betty Crocker Pizza Crust Mix)
- 1 tablespoon olive oil
- ½ cup tomato sauce (use Contadina's pack-friendly Pizza Squeeze bottle)
- 1 4-ounce pouch pepperoni slices
- 1 tablespoon Italian seasoning

At home: Transfer Italian seasoning to ziplock bag. Pack oil in a leakproof container.

In camp: Finely dice cheese. In a bowl, combine baking mix and $1/2$ cup water; stir until dough forms. Pour oil into a 10-inch skillet. Roll dough thin on a plate with a rigid plastic water bottle and transfer to skillet (or spread it evenly across skillet with a spoon). Top with tomato sauce, cheese, and pepperoni. Cover the pizza with a pot lid and cook over medium heat for 5 minutes, or until cheese melts. Top with Italian seasoning.

(serves 2)

Variations: Try these variations to make more great pizza!

» Greek: feta cheese + chopped olives + chopped pepperoncinis
» Spicy Southwest: pepper jack cheese + black beans + chili powder
» Vegan: soy mozzarella + chopped portobello mushrooms + broccoli
» Purely Potent: Gorgonzola cheese + chopped garlic + anchovies
» Dessert Pizza: Nutella + dried strawberries + walnuts

Reader's Tip
Take whole-wheat pitas and make pizzas on them—that way, you don't end up with sticky hands or doughy centers! They are super yummy and make pizzas super fast.

Chef's Secret

Make sure your pizza doesn't burn by spreading the dough thinly and removing it from the heat as soon as the cheese is melted. You might be wondering why we don't suggest using preshredded mozzarella (or another soft variety)—that's because the harder a cheese is, the longer it'll last in the backcountry. And if you leave it in block form and dice right before baking (rather than shredding ahead of time), it'll stay fresh even longer.

If your cheese is slow to melt and the dough is cooked through, add a few drops of water to the hot skillet and cover quickly with your lid. The steam will help melt your cheese.

Parmesan Polenta Pizza

Improve the basic pie with cornmeal crust and fresh basil sauce.

1 ounce dried porcini mushrooms

2 ounces dried bell peppers

5-ounce block Asiago cheese

20 cherry tomatoes

3 ounces dried salami

2 tablespoons olive oil

2 sprigs fresh basil

1 cup instant polenta (coarse cornmeal)

1 teaspoon salt

$1/3$ cup grated Parmesan cheese

At home: Place polenta and salt in one ziplock bag and Parmesan in another. Slice salami and pack in a third ziplock bag. Chop basil, mix with oil, and pour into a leakproof container. Keep tomatoes in the original plastic container, but fill empty space with balled-up paper towels to keep them from getting squished in your pack.

In camp: Place mushrooms and peppers in a bowl, cover with water for 30 minutes, then drain. Finely dice Asiago cheese. To make sauce, quarter tomatoes and place in a 10-inch skillet with salami and the olive oil/basil mix. Cook over medium heat for 2 minutes, pressing on tomatoes with a spatula to break them down. Remove from skillet and place in a bowl. Mix polenta and salt in another bowl with Parmesan and 1 cup water; spread dough thinly across skillet. Top with sauce, cheese, mushrooms, and peppers. Cover and cook over medium heat for 5 to 7 minutes, until crust is crisp and browned.

(serves 2)

PERFECT PASTA DISHES

Kickin' Mac and Cheese

Fast, filling, and yummy macaroni and cheese is comfort food wherever you pitch your tent.

1 pound pasta

4 tablespoons powdered milk

Red pepper flakes to taste

Garlic powder to taste

1 cup or more (depending on preference) diced
    sharp cheddar cheese

3–4 tablespoons butter or margarine

Salt and pepper to taste

At home: Put butter in a hard container. Place powdered milk, red pepper flakes, garlic, salt, and pepper in separate ziplock bags.

In camp: Boil water and add pasta; cook until done (about 8 to 12 minutes). Stir occasionally to keep the noodles from sticking. Meanwhile, rehydrate powdered milk following package directions (add enough water to give it the consistency of milk). Once the pasta is done, remove it from heat. Drain water. Add milk, red pepper flakes, and garlic powder; stir to coat pasta. For a creamier mac, use more milk. Mix in cheese and butter. Return pot to stove, and heat slowly, stirring constantly until cheese melts. Add salt and pepper to taste.

(serves 3)

Eight Tips for Making Pasta

Easy to cook and packed with carbohydrates, noodles are ideal for helping you refuel after a long day on the trail.

1. Use at least 1 quart (4 cups) of water for every 4 ounces of dry pasta. Plenty of water will help prevent the pasta from clumping and sticking together.

2. Cover the pot with a lid to help bring the water to a boil faster. This doesn't mean that the water won't boil over, so be sure to watch it.

3. Salt the water to boost the pasta's flavor. Use a maximum 2 tablespoons of salt per pound of pasta. Do not add salt until the water comes to a boil. If you add the salt to cold water, it will take a little longer for the water to boil and the salt could also pit the bottom of your pot.

4. Stir the pasta after you add it to the boiling water and occasionally throughout the cooking process. This will prevent noodles from clumping and sticking to the bottom of the pot.

5. Don't add oil to the water. Oil will coat the pasta and prevent your sauce from sticking.

6. Pasta can overcook quickly. Test for doneness about 4 minutes before the time given on the package instructions. Most pastas cook in approximately 8 to 12 minutes. Noodles should be tender but still firm, or al dente. Remember that pasta will continue to cook and soften even after you drain it. For fresh pasta, you know it is done when it rises to the surface.

7. Drain the pasta immediately in a large colander and shake it well to remove excess water. Don't rinse the pasta (except when making a cold pasta salad or lasagna). Rinsing the pasta will remove the starch that helps your sauce adhere to the noodles.

8. Try whole-wheat or whole-grain pasta. It has more fiber, which will keep you fuller longer.

Pine Nut Pasta

You can enjoy the taste of fresh ingredients with this homemade pesto recipe.

2 packed cups fresh basil leaves

$1/2$ cup grated Parmesan cheese

$1/2$ teaspoon salt

1 clove garlic

$1/4$ cup pine nuts

Red pepper flakes (optional)

$2/3$ cup extra-virgin olive oil

Sun-dried tomatoes (optional)

1 pound pasta such as rotini, bow tie, penne,
or angel hair

At home: In a food processor, combine basil, Parmesan cheese, and salt. Add garlic, pine nuts, and, if you want some added kick to your sauce, red pepper flakes. (If you don't have any pine nuts handy, you can also use walnuts.) Once all of the ingredients are combined, slowly add extra-virgin olive oil. Adjust the sauce to your taste. Some people like their sauce smoother with a little more olive oil, while others prefer an earthier texture with more basil and pine nuts. Pack in a leakproof container. Pesto can go "off" and turn brown very quickly when exposed to air. A piece of plastic wrap pressed on top of packed pesto helps, as does topping the container with some olive oil. You can also store it in a small ziplock bag, partially zip it shut, and then suck the air out of it before sealing it completely. You can buy premade pesto sauce at the grocery store, but most cannot compete with homemade.

In camp: Cook pasta according to directions and tips listed on page 51. Drain pasta well and add pesto sauce. Mix well so all of the pasta is coated with sauce. If you have extra whole pine nuts or walnuts, you can sprinkle them on top. For added flavor, mix in some sun-dried tomatoes.

(serves 3)

Note: Toast the pine nuts or walnuts before adding to the pesto to enhance their flavor.

Cheesy Sausage Pasta

Vary ingredient amounts to taste.

Handful of sun-dried tomatoes
Handful of dried mushrooms of choice
1 4-ounce pouch Knorr-Lipton Four Cheese Bow Tie
     Italian Sides
1 chunk Gruyère cheese
1 chunk summer sausage

At home: Pack the tomatoes and mushrooms in a ziplock bag.

In camp: Rehydrate the dried ingredients in hot water for 20 to 30 minutes, or until soft. Drain. Cook pasta according to package directions. While pasta cooks, dice cheese and chop sausage into bite-size chunks. Add cheese, sausage, tomatoes, and mushrooms to pasta. Stir until cheese melts.

(serves 1)

Salmon-Studded Spaghetti

Pink salmon is the star of this pasta dish from the Pacific Northwest.

10 ounces spaghetti or other pasta

1 14-ounce can artichoke hearts, drained and
   quartered

1 tablespoon capers, drained and chopped

2 cloves garlic, minced

1 16-ounce foil pouch pink or smoked salmon

2 tablespoons olive oil

¼ cup Italian-style bread crumbs

¼ cup grated Parmesan cheese

At home: Place artichoke hearts, capers, and garlic in a zip-lock bag.

In camp: Cook pasta according to package directions; drain. Meanwhile, in a separate skillet, sauté artichoke hearts, capers, garlic, and salmon in oil until heated through. Toss with pasta and bread crumbs, and top with cheese.

(serves 2)

Chef's Secret

Foil packs of chicken, salmon, and tuna can be found in most grocery stores in the canned-meat section. As long as the packs are unopened, the meat is shelf-stable and can be stored indefinitely.

Alpine Pasta

You want to eat gourmet but have only ten minutes to shop. Solution: This pasta dish featuring salami and diced sun-dried tomatoes.

    2 ounces sun-dried tomatoes
    2 4.4-ounce Knorr Butter & Herb pasta
        packets
    4 ounces pepper-coated salami, diced
    6 green onions, chopped
    5 ounces Gruyère cheese, grated

In camp: Boil a cup of water and pour it over tomatoes. In a separate pot, cook pasta according to package instructions. While pasta simmers, chop softened tomatoes. After pasta cooks for 5 minutes, add all ingredients and stir until noodles are done.

(serves 2)

Pasta with Herbes de Provence

A special spice mix to bring the taste of France into your backcountry kitchen.

    4–5 ounces canned, dehydrated, or pouch pre-
        cooked chicken
    3 large sun-dried tomatoes

1 cup dried mushrooms

3 ounces angel hair pasta

1 large clove garlic

¼ cup olive oil

2 tablespoons herbes de Provence

1 tablespoon grated Parmesan cheese (use one of
    the packets from your last pizza delivery)

At home: Place herbs, tomatoes, mushrooms, and cheese in separate ziplock bags. Pecooked chicken usually comes in some kind of packable container such as a foil pouch or a can. Place olive oil in a small plastic bottle, and pack garlic and pasta in another ziplock bag.

In camp: Thirty to 60 minutes before eating, bring water to a boil. If you're using dehydrated chicken, let it sit, covered, in the hot water for the full hour to rehydrate. If not, let the tomatoes and mushrooms rehydrate for 20 to 30 minutes in the hot water. When ready to really start cooking, boil pasta in water for 4 minutes, then drain and remove from pot. Finely dice garlic, then heat in the pot with olive oil, drained tomatoes, and drained mushrooms until garlic is lightly toasted. Add chicken to the pot and stir until well-mixed. Top with herbs and Parmesan.

(serves 1)

FANCY FISH FEASTS

Cold-water trout contains healthy doses of omega-3 fatty acids and protein, This means that, while the catching is fun and the eating is great, the fish is good for you!

Mediterranean Stuffed Trout

Lemons and olives deliver a flavorful punch.

1 lemon
$^1/_3$ cup oil-cured olives
2 cleaned whole trout
1 cup flour
$^1/_2$ teaspoon salt
1 teaspoon lemon pepper
1 teaspoon dried thyme
1 tablespoon cooking oil

At home: Combine flour, salt, and lemon pepper in a gallon-size ziplock bag.

In camp: Slice lemon into $^1/_2$-inch sections and set aside. Slice olives. Place trout in the ziplock bag containing flour, salt, and lemon pepper; toss gently to coat. Sprinkle the inside of the fish with thyme, and cover with lemon and olive slices. Heat oil in pan to sizzling and cook trout until flesh is flaky. To keep your trout from curling when frying, score the skin.

(serves 2)

Whole Trout with Cranberry-Almond Sauce

Crunchy and flavorful, this gourmet dish is the trail mix of fish recipes.

   1/4 cup dried cranberries
   2 cleaned whole trout
   1 cup flour
   1/2 teaspoon salt
   1/4 teaspoon ground black pepper
   Pinch of cayenne pepper
   Pinch of ground cinnamon
   1 tablespoon cooking oil
   1/4 cup minced onion
   1/3 cup chopped toasted almonds
   1 tablespoon butter (optional)

At home: Combine flour, salt, black pepper, cayenne, and cinnamon in a gallon-size ziplock bag. Store cranberries, almonds, and onions separately.

In camp: Soak cranberries in 1 cup of water for 5 minutes to soften. Place trout in bag with flour and spices, and toss to coat. Heat oil in pan to sizzling and fry trout until flesh is flaky (3 to 6 minutes per side, depending on size of fish). Simultaneously, make sauce: Add onions to pan and sauté 30 seconds. Add almonds, cranberries, and their water (and butter, if using) and stir to combine. Pour sauce over cooked trout.

(serves 2)

Pack-a-Fish Kit

For most fish dinners, you'll need a few basic supplies for cleaning and cooking:

- 10-inch frying pan (nonstick coatings speed cleanup)
- Plastic spatula
- Pocketknife or multitool with knife for filleting fish. If you anticipate catching big fish (12 inches or more), pack a 6-inch fillet knife.
- Olive oil packed in leakproof container
- And to accompany your trout, plan on a side dish such as flavored rice. We like Lipton's Creamy Garlic Parmesan, and Herb and Butter.

Smoked Trout with White Wine Sauce

Not catching any fish? You can still enjoy the flavor and nutritional benefits of fish with vacuum-sealed foil packets containing trout or salmon.

1/2 pound dehydrated portobello mushrooms
(or other dried mushrooms)

1 dehydrated red bell pepper

4 tablespoons olive oil

2 cloves garlic, chopped

Salt and black pepper to taste

1 bay leaf

1/2 cup white wine (To wine and dine, CalNaturale makes an awesome, affordable boxed chardonnay; www.calnaturale.com.)

Several sprigs of rosemary
Several leaves of sweet basil
1 teaspoon potato flour
1 8-ounce vacuum-packed smoked trout or salmon

At home: Put dry ingredients in separate ziplock bags. Place olive oil in a leakproof container.

In camp: Rehydrate mushrooms and bell pepper by soaking them in hot water, covered, for 5 to 10 minutes. Heat oil in a pot and sauté mushrooms and garlic until tender. Add bell pepper and also cook until tender. Mix in salt, pepper, and bay leaf. Add white wine, tear in rosemary and sweet basil, and simmer about 6 minutes. Mix in potato flour to thicken, then add trout or salmon and heat for about 2 minutes.

Trout with Mustard Sauce

This thick, tangy topping dresses up any fish.

- 1 tablespoon cooking oil
- 4 trout fillets
- 1 cup water
- 1/4 cup butter (or 4 tablespoons olive oil)
- 1 package McCormick hollandaise sauce mix
- 1 tablespoon Dijon mustard
- 1 teaspoon dried tarragon

In camp: Heat oil in pan to sizzling and cook trout until flesh is flaky. To make sauce, fork-whisk water, butter (or olive oil), and contents of sauce packet. Add mustard and tarragon, and bring to a boil. Pour sauce over trout.

(serves 2)

Spicy Southwest Trout

Give your fish a kick with green chilies and cornmeal.

- 2 cleaned whole trout
- 1 cup cornmeal
- 1 teaspoon mild chili powder
- 1/2 teaspoon salt
- 1/4 teaspoon pepper
- 2 tablespoons cooking oil
- 1/4 cup minced onion
- 1 4-ounce can chopped green chilies

Three Ways to Cook Trout without a Pan

If you forgot your fish kit but caught the fish, you can still enjoy a yummy trout dinner without a pan.

Baked: Make a campfire and get a good bed of coals going. Place a thin, flat rock on the coals, pizza oven–style. Bank coals around the rock. Clean the trout, brush it with olive oil, and cook, flipping a few times until done.

Grilled: Weave together green branches to make an improvised grill. Set the grill on rocks over your fire and cook—just be sure to remove the fish if the branches start to burn.

Ceviche: Clean trout and chop into 1-inch pieces. Place in a ziplock bag filled with fresh lemon or lime juice (use 6 fruits per pound of fish). Chill in a snowbank or cold pond for 4 to 6 hours, stirring after the first hour.

At home: Combine cornmeal, chili powder, salt, and pepper in a gallon-size ziplock bag.

In camp: Place trout in the bag with flour and spices, and toss to coat. Heat oil in pan to sizzling and fry trout until flesh is flaky. Remove trout and keep warm. Add onion to pan and sauté 30 seconds. Stir in chilies and serve over trout.

(serves 2)

HEARTY ONE-POT STEWS

Chicken and Dumplings

This simple one-pot meal can be made from leftovers you bring from home.

1 tablespoon chicken bouillon
1 tablespoon dried veggie flakes
1 tablespoon dried onion flakes
$1/2$ teaspoon celery salt
$1/4$ teaspoon black pepper
$1/4$ teaspoon dried thyme
7 ounces leftover chicken
$2 1/4$ cups Bisquick
1 teaspoon dried parsley

At home: Put the first six ingredients in a ziplock bag. Freeze the chicken in a second bag. Put the Bisquick and parsley in a third bag.

In camp: Boil 3 cups water, add contents of first bag, and simmer. Slice and add chicken. Make dumplings by adding $2/3$ cup water to Bisquick bag. Seal and squish to mix. Snip off corner of bag and squeeze dough into soup. Cover until dumplings float to top.

(serves 2)

Mushroom Soup with Gremolata

An Italian-style relish adds the robust taste of garlic, parsley, and lemon to your basic mushroom soup.

1 small garlic clove, minced
1 tablespoon finely chopped fresh parsley
    (or 1 teaspoon dried)
1 teaspoon lemon zest
3 cups dried mushrooms (cremini, shiitake, oyster,
    or white)
2 tablespoons olive oil
3 tablespoons flour
4 cups water
4 chicken bouillon cubes
Salt and pepper to taste
3 green onions

At home: Put lemon zest in a ziplock bag.

Reader's Tip

Okay, crazy as this sounds, snowshoe or winter hiking trips are the perfect opportunity for broth-cicles! You can save time by freezing soup in an ice-cube tray (figure $1/2$ tray makes $1/2$ cup), then hauling the cubes sealed in a ziplock bag into the backcountry. Put an inch or so of water in your pan as a starter, drop in the broth cubes, and you'll have a tasty meal in minutes. Saves you time, and you don't have to pack seasonings if you season the broth before freezing.

Chef's Secret

You don't have to rehydrate the mushrooms before sautéing them; they'll rehydrate in the broth as you cook the soup. However, if you prefer, you can let the mushrooms soak for 15 minutes in cool water before you begin cooking.

In camp: To make the gremolata, combine minced garlic, parsley, and lemon zest; set aside. For the soup, slice mushrooms and add to a pot with the olive oil. Sauté for 5 minutes. Add flour, stirring for 2 to 3 minutes or until flour browns slightly. Gradually add water and stir until smooth. Add bouillon cubes, heat to a boil, and simmer 5 minutes. Season with salt and pepper. Slice green onions and add to the pot. Spoon soup into bowls and garnish with gremolata.

(serves 2–3)

Double Onion and Potato Stew

A crispy, cheesy garnish tops this winter comfort dish.

4 cups water
2 tablespoons cornstarch
1 cup dried potatoes
4 beef bouillon cubes
$1/4$ teaspoon dried thyme
1 medium onion
1 tablespoon chopped fresh parsley (or 1 teaspoon
    dried)
Salt and pepper to taste
$3/4$ cup shredded Parmesan cheese
$1/2$ cup French-fried onions (such as French's)

At home: Place potatoes, bouillon cubes, and thyme in a zip-lock bag.

In camp: Put water in a pot and stir in cornstarch until smooth. Place over high heat. Add potato mixture, heat to boiling, and simmer for 6 to 7 minutes. Thinly slice onion and add to the pot. Simmer 5 more minutes. Season with parsley, salt, and pepper. Spoon stew into bowls and garnish with Parmesan cheese and French-fried onions.

(serves 2)

Moroccan Fish Tagine

Whip up the trail version of a classic North African slow-cooked stew.

1 6-ounce can tomato paste
4 cups water
¼ cup red lentils
¼ cup split peas
½ teaspoon ground ginger
½ teaspoon paprika
1 teaspoon ground cinnamon
1 7-ounce pouch chunk salmon or tuna
1 apple
½ cup sliced almonds
½ cup raisins or chopped prunes
Salt and pepper to taste
Juice from 1 lemon (optional)

At home: Place lentils, peas, ginger, paprika, and cinnamon in a ziplock bag.

In camp: In a pot, combine tomato paste and water and then add lentil mixture. Heat to boiling and simmer 10 to 15 minutes. Add salmon or tuna and cook for 3 to 4 minutes, or until lentils and peas are tender. Chop apple into bite-size pieces and add to the pot with almonds and raisins or prunes. Season with salt and pepper. Remove from heat and garnish with lemon juice.

(serves 2–3)

PORTABLE PUB GRUB

Mushroom-Asiago Veggie Burgers

Okay, it's not beef, but there's still something very satisfying about a burger, veggie or not.

   1 cup (6 ounces) veggie burger mix
   1 cup boiling water
   2 large cremini mushrooms
   $^1/_2$ cup grated Asiago cheese

Olive oil (optional)

4 large burger buns

Condiments such as mayo, ketchup, mustard, lettuce, onion, and tomato

At home: Pack buns in your cook pot or a smash-proof plastic container. Do not dice or wash mushrooms, as this can accelerate spoilage.

In camp: Place burger mix in a heat-safe bowl. Add boiling water, stir, and let stand for 10 to 15 minutes, or until mixture is cooled and set. Dice mushrooms and work into mix along with cheese. Form into 4 patties. Pan-fry in a nonstick skillet (with olive oil, if using). Fry each side until browned and burger is cooked through. Place on bun and add fixings.

(serves 4)

Spicy Sweet Potato Fries

Backcountry fare tends toward one-pot glop meals. So if you are looking for something crispy, try these fries.

  2–3 medium sweet potatoes
  Olive or canola oil
  1–2 teaspoon sea salt
  Seasonings such as onion powder, Italian seasoning,
      and/or seasoning salt

At home: Place potatoes in paper bag.

In camp: Peel sweet potatoes, then cut into 2-inch strips. Coat a large skillet with oil. In batches, add sweet potatoes and sprinkle with sea salt and seasonings. Fry until browned on both sides, about 10 to 15 minutes. Remove to a plate and top with additional seasonings, if desired.

(serves 4–6)

Chef's Secret

To bake fries, wrap them in foil along with the seasonings and place the packet directly on hot coals, omit the oil.

Hot Spinach and Artichoke Dip

If your meal takes more than five minutes to cook and you have a lot of hungry campers eager to chow, try serving this tantalizing appetizer to tide people over.

1 5-ounce can evaporated milk

1 tablespoon cornstarch

¼ teaspoon salt

1 12-ounce jar quartered and marinated artichoke
　　　hearts, chopped (we like Cento's)

2 cups fresh baby spinach, lightly chopped

2–3 tablespoons chopped fresh basil

¾ cup grated Parmesan and Romano cheese blend

At home: Place spinach, basil, and cheese in a large ziplock bag.

In camp: Whisk evaporated milk, cornstarch, and salt in a medium saucepan until smooth. Place over medium heat, stirring frequently until thick and bubbly. Remove from heat; add artichoke hearts, spinach, basil, and cheese. Stir and return to heat for 6 to 7 minutes or until spinach is wilted and cheese is melted. For dipping, pack a bag of pita chips (they're less fragile than other chips) or a loaf of crusty bread, or make tortilla chips in camp (see page 75).

(serves 4–6)

Toasted Tortilla Chips

Chips turn into dust in your backpack, so your best bet is to make your own on the spot.

4 10-inch tortillas (try Mission's Garden Spinach
Herb or Jalapeño and Cheddar)
2 tablespoons olive or canola oil (optional)
Pinch of sea salt

At home: Cut tortillas into wedges and place in a ziplock bag.

In camp: Fry tortilla wedges in a skillet with oil until crisp and browned, or use a dry nonstick skillet. Remove from heat and sprinkle lightly with sea salt.

(serves 4–6)

BACKCOUNTRY JAPANESE NIGHT

Rice and Egg Domburi

Pack in the protein with this hearty bowl of food.

2 cups cooked rice (use instant rice pouches, if you
prefer, to get quantity desired)
1 small sweet potato
1 3-ounce pouch Chicken of the Sea Smoked Pacific
Salmon
1 3-ounce package powdered eggs
3 tablespoons Japanese rice vinegar
2 tablespoons plain white sugar
2 teaspoons salt

At home: Pack potato in paper bag. Place rice vinegar, sugar, and salt in a small plastic container. Shake to dissolve sugar and salt.

In camp: Cook rice according to instructions, let cool in serving bowls. Cut potato and salmon into ¼-inch cubes. Add water to powdered eggs per package directions and fry with potato in a small pan over medium heat until all are cooked (about 10 minutes). Add salmon with about a minute to go. Serve over hot rice, adding rice vinegar mixture for flavor.

(serves 2)

Pink Caterpillar Rolls

Tart strawberries and creamy avocado fill this tasty roll.

- 2 cups cooked rice (use instant rice pouches, if you prefer, to get quantity desired)
- 2 sheets nori, a dark-green, paper-thin sheet of shredded sea vegetables used to roll sushi
- 10-inch-square sushi mat (weighs only 2 ounces)
- 3 tablespoons Japanese rice vinegar
- 2 tablespoons plain white sugar
- 2 teaspoons salt
- 1 firm avocado, sliced into long, narrow strips
- ½ cup strawberries (dried or fresh)
- 1 2-ounce pouch albacore tuna

At home: Place rice vinegar, sugar, and salt in a small plastic container. Shake until sugar and salt are dissolved. Pack avocado in a paper bag.

In camp: Cook rice according to package directions. Let it cool. Lay nori on rough side of sushi mat and line up evenly. Press wet, clean fingers over nori until it's damp. Cover nori sheet with a thin layer of rice. Drizzle rice with vinegar mixture to make sticky. Place avocado strips on center of nori in a single horizontal line, making sure line goes to edges of nori. Arrange 7 or 8 strawberries above avocado. Below avocado, create another horizontal line with 1½ tablespoons of tuna. Lift bottom edge of mat and fold once, pressing firmly. Pull mat off top of the sushi and repeat until the roll is complete. Form the roll into a circle or square using the mat. Repeat process for second roll.

(serves 2)

Macho Miso

Carrots, daikon, and shiitake mushrooms add heft to this nutritious soup.

    1 carrot
    1 daikon radish
    5 small shiitake mushrooms
    1⅓ cups water
    2 ⅕-ounce pouches tofu miso soup mix

At home: Combine carrot and daikon in a ziplock bag. Pack mushrooms in a small plastic container.

In camp: Slice carrot and daikon. Add mushrooms, carrot, and daikon to water, boil for 5 minutes. Add miso soup mix.

(serves 2)

Sesame White-Bean Potato Cakes

These potato cakes are heavy on the carbs and taste.

- 1 15-ounce can great northern beans
- 1 1/2 cups instant potato flakes
- 2 teaspoons powdered milk
- 2 tablespoons onion soup mix
- 1 cup cold water
- 4 tablespoons sesame seeds
- 4 tablespoons olive oil

At home: Drain and rinse beans, then double-bag in ziplock bags.

In camp: Smash beans into a paste with a spoon. Combine potato flakes, powdered milk, and soup mix. Mix with bean paste and water. Shape dough into 8 balls and flatten each into a 1-inch-thick patty. Pour sesame seeds in a shallow plate; press each patty firmly into the seeds to coat both sides. Heat oil in a skillet and cook patties about 3 minutes per side, until golden brown.

(serves 4)

Reader's Tip

To save weight, make your own dehydrated white bean paste at home, or use Instant Black Beans or Instant Refried Beans from Fantastic Foods; www.fantastic foods.com.

Italian-Style Potatoes

Spice up boring potatoes with summer sausage, brown sugar, and tomatoes in this Italian-inspired dish.

¹/₄ cup diced onion

1 tablespoon olive oil

1 teaspoon brown sugar

¹/₂ cup (about 2.5 ounces) diced summer sausage

2 cups water

¹/₄ cup chopped sun-dried tomatoes

1¹/₂ cups instant potato flakes

¹/₂ teaspoon salt

3 tablespoons grated Parmesan cheese

In camp: Sauté onions in oil over medium-high heat until translucent. Add sugar and stir. Add sausage and sauté until browned,

then remove from heat. Bring water to a boil; pour $1/2$ cup over tomatoes in a bowl and let soak 5 minutes. Return sausage and onions to heat, stirring until warm. In another pot, mix potatoes, salt, and remaining water until smooth. Drain tomatoes and add to skillet with sausage; sauté 1 to 2 minutes. Remove from heat and stir in cheese. Serve over potato mixture.

(serves 2)

Wasabi Potatoes with Salmon

The wasabi adds a kick to instant potatoes, while the salmon is a perfect protein source.

$1^{1}/_{2}$ cups water
$1^{1}/_{2}$ cups instant potato flakes
2 teaspoons wasabi powder (check the Asian
    section of your grocery store)
1 6-ounce pouch salmon

At home: Pack potato flakes and wasabi powder together in a ziplock bag.

In camp: Bring water to a simmer. Add the potato-wasabi mix and stir until smooth. Remove from heat, add salmon, and serve.

(serves 2)

OLYMPIC FEAST

Greek Beef

For a fun alternative to the normal cheese and pasta backcountry dinner, go Greek.

1 cup bread crumbs

1/4 cup whole milk

1/4 cup crumbled feta cheese

1/4 cup minced fresh parsley

2 tablespoons chopped green onions

2 teaspoons dried oregano

1 egg, slightly beaten

1 pound lean ground beef or ground chuck

1–2 tablespoons olive oil

1 tablespoon minced garlic

1/4 teaspoon red pepper flakes

1/2 cup sliced kalamata olives

At home: Mix the first seven ingredients well in a bowl. Add beef and thoroughly mix together. In a large frying pan, heat a tablespoon or two of olive oil over medium-high. When heated, sauté garlic, red pepper flakes, and olives for 2 minutes, then add beef mixture. Cook beef thoroughly, drain, and dry in a dehydrator at 120ºF. (Time depends on your model of dehydrator.) A low-temp slow-dry works better for this mixture due to the feta cheese.

In camp: To rehydrate mixture, pour in enough boiling water to cover mixture plus about ¼ inch extra. Wrap pot in a sleeping bag or coat and let sit for 15 minutes until mixture is rehydrated.

(serves 4)

Lemon Couscous

Accompany your Greek Beef with this lemony couscous recipe for a delicious and authentic Olympic taste.

- ¾ cup chicken broth (1 bouillon cube and ¾ cup water)
- 1 tablespoon olive oil
- ¼ cup water and 6 True Lemon packets, or ¼ cup lemon juice
- ¾ cup dry plain couscous

At home: Package couscous in a ziplock bag.

In camp: Bring chicken broth, olive oil, and lemon water (or lemon juice) to a boil, then add to couscous. Let sit for 5 minutes.

(serves 3)

Feta Yogurt Sauce

And for the final touch for your Olympic feast: the sauce.

¼ cup crumbled feta cheese
¼ cup plain yogurt
2 tablespoons lemon juice, or 2 True Lemon packets
¼ teaspoon black pepper

At home: Mix together the ingredients and pack in a leak-proof plastic container. Yogurt-based sauce will stay fresh for a couple of days.

In camp: Pour over meat and couscous and enjoy.

(serves 3–4)

CURRY VARIATIONS

Masman Curry

Lemongrass and peanuts accent this creamy Thai dish.

1 4-ounce pouch instant mashed potatoes

1 tablespoon Masman curry paste (contains lemongrass, garlic, cumin available at www.tastepad
thai.com and www.pacificrimgourmet.com)

1 1.75-ounce pouch coconut cream powder
(available at Asian or Indian groceries) and
1 cup water, or 1 cup canned coconut milk

$1/2$ medium onion, peeled and thinly sliced

$1/2$ cup matchstick-cut carrots

1 tablespoon brown sugar

$1/3$ cup crushed peanuts

1 7-ounce pouch precooked chicken breast
(vegetarian option: 1 14-ounce can chickpeas)

At home: Combine brown sugar and crushed peanuts in a ziplock bag. If using chickpeas, place in a separate ziplock bag. Place precut onions and carrots in two more ziplock bags.

In camp: Prepare potatoes according to package directions; set aside. In a separate pot, combine curry with coconut powder and water (or canned coconut milk). Bring to a boil. Add onions and carrots and cook, stirring, for 3 minutes. Add sugar, nuts, and chicken (or chickpeas), and cook until sugar is dissolved and everything is hot. Spread over potatoes.

(serves 2)

Spicy—and Ultralight—Curried Noodles

Lighten your load and still eat like a king or queen with this ultralight meal, courtesy of Backpacker *magazine's discriminating gear editor, Kristin Hostetter. As she puts it: "It requires a bit of upfront prep work at home, but pretty much zero work in camp. It's superlight (just six ounces per serving!) and, man, does it taste good! Way better than anything prepackaged." The secret: dehydrated ingredients + a freezer bag.*

- 1 serving of Asian cellophane noodles (They typically come in large bricks. Break off a chunk about 3 by 6 inches.)
- ¼ cup dehydrated meat of your choice (burger or chicken)
- ¼ cup dehydrated mixed veggies
- 1 tablespoon curry
- 1 tablespoon cumin
- 1 tablespoon coriander
- 1 tablespoon garam masala
- ½ teaspoon ground ginger
- 2 tablespoons coconut cream powder
- 2 tablespoons powdered milk
- Dash of cayenne
- Salt and pepper to taste
- Handful of cashews

At home: Combine all ingredients except the cashews in a quart-size ziplock bag.

In camp: Add about 1½ cups boiling water to a plastic bag. Squish it around and wrap it in a coat or sleeping bag for about 10 minutes, or until everything is tender. Top with cashews.

(serves 1)

Caribbean Pineapple Curry

Give your camp dinner a tropical flair.

1¹/₂ ounces of rum (use a mini bottle or measure and
place in leakproof container) (optional)

1 7-ounce pouch precooked
chicken breast
(optional)

1¹/₂ cups instant rice
1 tablespoon vegetable oil
1 jalapeño, seeded and
sliced
1 clove garlic, chopped
¹/₂ onion, peeled and sliced
1 cup julienned red bell
pepper
1 teaspoon curry powder
1 snack-size (4-ounce) container pineapple chunks

At home: Combine jalapeño and garlic in a ziplock bag.

In camp: If using chicken and rum, add rum to chicken
pouch and set aside to marinate. Boil 1¹/₂ cups water, stir in
rice, and cover. Cook until water is absorbed, follow package
instructions for instant rice (usually takes approximately 90
seconds). In a separate pot, heat oil and fry jalapeño and
garlic for 30 seconds. Add onion, pepper, and curry. Stir for 3
minutes, or until veggies soften. Add pineapple and optional
chicken and rum, and cook till heated through. Pour over rice.

(serves 2)

Thai Green Curry

This sweet-tasting dish is more fragrant than spicy.

6 ounces rice noodles or linguine

2 teaspoons green curry paste

1 tablespoon brown sugar

1 1.75-ounce pouch coconut
     cream powder (available
     at Asian and Indian grocer-
     ies) and 1 cup water, or 1
     cup canned coconut milk

$^{1}/_{2}$ small onion, peeled and
     thinly sliced

$^{1}/_{2}$ cup matchstick-cut carrots

2 3.5-ounce pouches precooked
     shrimp (vegetarian option:
     1 12-ounce package firm
     tofu, cut into 1-inch cubes)

$^{1}/_{2}$ lime (optional)

$^{1}/_{4}$ cup chopped cilantro
     (optional)

In camp: Cook noodles according to package directions, drain, and set aside. In a separate pot, combine curry and brown sugar with coconut powder and water (or canned milk) and bring to a boil. Add onions and carrots and cook (while stirring) for 3 minutes. Stir in shrimp (or tofu) and cook till heated through. Serve over noodles and add lime or cilantro if desired.

(serves 2)

WILD EDIBLES

Early spring roots are packed with nutrients, says naturalist and author "Wildman" Steve Brill, who teaches people how to find and feast on wild plants. He created the following recipes featuring roots common to most forest trails. Not into foraging? All three meals are easily prepared with grocery-store substitutes.

Baked Wild Parsnips

A crunchy side dish for soup or pasta.

> 3 cups coarsely sliced wild (or regular) parsnips
> 1/2 teaspoon dried thyme
> 1/2 teaspoon dried rosemary
> Dash of cayenne hot pepper, or 1/4 teaspoon black
>   pepper
> 1/4 teaspoon salt
> 2 tablespoons vegetable oil
> 1 tablespoon balsamic vinegar

At home: Combine thyme, rosemary, cayenne, and salt in a ziplock bag. Stash vegetable oil and vinegar in a leakproof plastic container.

In camp: Mixed the sliced parsnips with the rest of the ingredients on a plate. Wrap the mixture in aluminum foil, place over hot coals, and bake 15 minutes, turning occasionally.

(serves 4)

The Flavorful Parsnip

Parsnip (*Pastinaca sativa*) is a root vegetable related to the carrot. Native to Eurasia, parsnips were brought to the United States by British colonists in the 1600s and were once one of the most important vegetables in the American diet. Parsnips are worth rediscovering, not only for their flavor and versatility, but also because they are abundant and in many states considered a noxious weed, so you can harvest them with abandon. Parsnips have a sweet flavor when cooked.

Basic Burdock Rice

This potato-like root soaks up salty spices.

$1/2$ cup thinly sliced ($1/16$-inch slices) burdock (or
  canned water chestnuts)
1 teaspoon dried thyme
1 teaspoon dried sage
1 teaspoon dried rosemary
1 tablespoon tamari soy sauce
1 tablespoon olive oil or other vegetable oil
2 vegetable bouillon cubes (for 2 cups of water)
1 cup instant brown rice, uncooked

Burdock

Burdock (*Arctium minus*) was brought to North America from Europe by early settlers and is now widespread throughout the United States. A biennial, burdock prefers disturbed areas such as roadsides, stream banks, abandoned farmsteads, and pastures. In its first year, the plant produces a rosette of large, heart-shaped leaves with wooly undersides. In the second year, a 5-foot bushy, flowering stem emerges. Burdock is best known for its seeds, which are covered with hooked bristles and are said to be the inspiration for Velcro. Burdock produces a fleshy taproot that is used as a food and for treating a variety of ailments including coughs, asthma, venereal disease, lung and skin disease, and scurvy.

At home: Combine dry ingredients in a ziplock bag. Pour wet ingredients into separate leakproof plastic containers.

In camp: Combine all the ingredients in a quart-size pot. Cover and simmer over low heat for 10 minutes or until the rice has absorbed all the liquid.

(serves 4)

Wild Carrot–Onion Soup

The untamed ancestor of the common carrot is sharply sweet and chewy.

- 4 cups sliced wild carrots (substitute: regular carrots)
- 3 vegetable bouillon cubes (for 3 cups of water)
- 2 tablespoons arrowroot or kudzu powder
- 1/2 cup dried onions
- 2 teaspoons dried parsley
- 1/2 teaspoon ground nutmeg
- 1/2 teaspoon turmeric
- 1/2 teaspoon black pepper
- 4 cloves garlic, chopped (or 1/2 teaspoon garlic powder)
- 2 tablespoons olive oil
- 2 tablespoons lemon juice

Wild Carrots

Wild carrot (*Daucus carota*), also called Queen Anne's lace, is an abundant nonnative member of the carrot family and is believed to have come over with early colonists in sacks of grain. The plant is now established throughout the United States. Wild carrot has a long, spindle-shaped taproot that is edible when young but gets tough and woody as it matures. The plant is said to sooth the digestive tract, support the liver, act as a diuretic, and stimulate the uterus. There is some belief that it can act as a kind of "morning after" pill, so pregnant women should use caution. All members of the carrot family can be mistaken for wild hemlock. Wild hemlock is poisonous, so care must be taken when cultivating wild carrots to ensure positive identification.

At home: Store dry ingredients in one ziplock bag and the bouillon in another. Stow olive oil and lemon juice in a small, leakproof plastic container.

In camp: Reconstitute the bouillon. Simmer all the ingredients together for 15 minutes, or until the carrots are tender.

(serves 4)

Easy Pad Thai

Ramen noodles have always been a go-to lightweight favorite of backpackers. You can up the ante and still enjoy the ease of instant noodles with this recipe, which transforms ramen from boring to exotic.

3 packages ramen noodles

1 7-ounce pouch precooked chicken breast

1/2 cup Asian sesame dressing (try Newman's Own Asian Sesame Natural Salad Mist, which comes in a pack-friendly 7-ounce plastic bottle)

1 cup shelled peanuts

At home: Crush peanuts into pieces with the bottom of a bowl or mug. Pack in a ziplock bag.

In camp: Cook ramen noodles according to package directions and drain (save the seasoning packet and add it to soup or rice later). Stir the chicken and dressing into the pot and cook for 1 minute. Sprinkle crushed peanuts over the noodles and serve.

(serves 3)

Reader's Tip

We love this! We have spent two months in Thailand in the last five years, and whether this tastes like "real" Pad Thai or not, it's quick, easy, and tastes great. It's easy to add whatever is handy to change it up a bit, such as ½ teaspoon crushed red pepper flakes or a different dressing.

Thai Red Curry Noodles with Soy Nuts

Curry adds exotic flavors to your next meal and can make you feel better, because one of its key ingredients—turmeric—reduces inflammation to ease post-hike aches.

2 cups water

2 packages ramen noodles

2 sugar packets

2 soy sauce packets

Half of a 1-ounce packet of SunBird's Thai Red Curry
    Seasoning Mix (more if you like it spicy)

1/2 cup soy nuts or peanuts (more if desired)

In camp: Bring water to a boil. Add ramen (excluding the spice packet), sugar, soy sauce, and SunBird seasoning mix. Simmer 2 to 3 minutes, or until noodles are tender. Add soy nuts and serve immediately.

(serves 2)

Chapter Four

Desserts

Okay, most of us don't get much beyond s'mores when we think about backcountry desserts, but there are lots of easy treats you can whip up to satisfy your sweet tooth that don't require a campfire or a lot of effort.

UPDATING THE CLASSICS

You know the basics: toast a marshmallow over the fire, place on a graham cracker with a square of chocolate, top with second graham cracker and enjoy. It's hard to imagine an improvement on this, but try one of these variations and you may be surprised.

The Johnny Appleseed

Apple-cinnamon graham crackers + marshmallow
+ apple slices

The Minty Fresh

Chocolate grahams + marshmallow + Andes mints

The Kindergarten Classic

Honey grahams + peanut butter + marshmallow + chocolate

The Tropical

Grahams + dried mango + marshmallow + coconut shavings

The Mexican S'more

Grahams + chili powder + cinnamon + marshmallow +
chocolate

The Inside-Out

Roast a marshmallow, then while it's still on the stick, roll it in
a shallow plate full of chocolate syrup and crushed graham
crackers.

FRUITY DESSERTS

Chocolate-Dipped Ginger and Mango

A sweet and savory dried-fruit dessert.

- 1 7-ounce package semisweet baking chocolate
- 2 tablespoons peanut oil
- 10 pieces crystallized ginger
- 10 slices dried mango

At home: Pour peanut oil into a small plastic bottle. Place
mango and ginger in a ziplock bag.

In camp: Fill a pan three-quarters full of water and place on stove over medium heat. Put chocolate in a metal cup or small pot and place in the pan of water (this prevents the chocolate from burning). Pour in peanut oil and stir until chocolate melts. Dip ginger and mango slices into chocolate, eating as a fondue.

(serves 2)

Campfire Baked Apples

Another variation on baked apples.

4 tart apples
$1/2$ cup raisins
$1/2$ cup unsweetened shredded coconut
$1/2$ cup brown sugar
1 teaspoon ground cinnamon
$1/2$ teaspoon ground nutmeg
Pinch of salt
4 teaspoons maple syrup

At home: Mix all the ingredients except the syrup and apples in a ziplock bag.

In camp: Core the apples. Fill each apple halfway with spoonfuls of the raisin-coconut-sugar-spice mixture. Add 1 teaspoon syrup to each apple, then top off with more mixture. Wrap apples individually in foil and bury in warm, ashy campfire coals for about 20 minutes or until apples are soft.

(serves 4)

Apple on a Stick

Here's a dessert that's kind of good for you. At least it has apples in it!

1 Jonathan or Rome apple for each person
$1/4$ cup granulated sugar per apple
1 teaspoon ground cinnamon per apple

At home: Combine sugar and cinnamon in a ziplock bag.

In camp: Push a stick or dowel through the apple top until the apple is secure on the stick. Place the apple 2 or 3 inches above the hot coals, and turn the apple while roasting it. As the apple cooks, the skin browns and the juice drips out. When the skin is loose, remove the apple from the fire, but leave it on the stick. Carefully peel the hot skin off. Roll the apple in the sugar-cinnamon mixture, then roast it some more over the coals, letting the mixture warm until it forms a glaze. Remove the apple from heat, let cool, and enjoy.

(serves 1)

Creamy Berry (or Peachy) Pie

An extra-special treat when the berries are ripe.

 2 cups water
 $^2/_3$ cup fresh berries (or chopped fresh peaches)
 $^2/_3$ cup powdered milk
 1 3$^1/_8$-ounce package instant vanilla pudding mix
 2 teaspoons vanilla powder
 2 teaspoons butter powder
 1 teaspoon ground cinnamon
 $^1/_2$ teaspoon ground nutmeg
 1 8-inch graham cracker piecrust
 Handful of fresh berries

At home: Combine the powdered milk, pudding mix, vanilla powder, butter powder, cinnamon, and nutmeg in a ziplock bag.

In camp: Boil water in a pot, then add berries. Cover the pot and let stand for 10 minutes, then cool for 10 minutes. Gradually add the pudding mixture while stirring. Pour the mixture into the piecrust and arrange extra berries on top. Let set for 5 minutes, then dig in.

(serves 4–8)

Coconut-Mango Rice Pudding

Try this with one of your curry dinners for an all-Asian meal.

- 2 teaspoons potato starch
- 8 tablespoons powdered milk
- 2 tablespoons coconut cream powder or powdered coconut
- 2 teaspoons sugar
- 4 tablespoons chopped dried mango (or dried fruit of your choice)
- 2 cups instant rice

At home: Combine all the ingredients in a ziplock bag. Shake to mix.

In camp: Divide dry mixture equally into four insulated mugs. Add boiling water to each mug. Stir well, cover, and wait 5 minutes before eating. Bonus: Makes a fine breakfast too, either as is, or add 4 tablespoons oatmeal to the dry ingredients for more texture and flavor.

(serves 4)

CAKES AND OTHER BAKED GOODIES

High-Country Poppy-Seed Cake

You can bake this yummy treat even at altitude, and you and your mates will be fighting over the last crumbs.

> 1 cup yellow cake mix
> 1 tablespoon powdered eggs
> 1 tablespoon whole poppy seeds
> 1 small oven bag

At home: Combine yellow cake mix, powdered eggs, and whole poppy seeds in a small oven bag. Mix well and close with a tie.

In camp: Add ¼ cup water to cake mix bag and squish well so there are no dry lumps. Tie the bag closed and form bag into a roughly circular shape that will fit nicely into your pot. Place the bag in a pot containing 1½ inches of boiling water. Lower heat to a simmer. Try to keep the bag in a horizontal position on the surface of the water. Bake 10 minutes and let stand for 3 minutes. Cut the bag open to allow steam to vent, then dig in!

(serves 4)

Variations: If you don't like poppy seeds, try 2 tablespoons chocolate chips or 1 tablespoon minced dried apricot and 2 tablespoons chopped pecans instead.

Muffins on the Trail

A creative way to bake muffins without an oven.

- 1 8.5-ounce package Jiffy Muffin Mix
- 1 2-quart pot with lid
- 1 3-quart pot with lid

In camp: Fill the bottom of the 2-quart pan with Jiffy Muffin Mix and mix with water according to package instructions. Now assemble your ultralight, improvised "Dutch oven." First, fill the bottom of the 3-quart pan with small rocks or gravel. Rocks or gravel should be about 1 inch deep throughout the pan. Next, place the 2-quart pan inside the 3-quart, on top of the rocks. The rocks will evenly spread the fire's heat to all sides of the 2-quart pan. Depending on the shape of your pans, you can either put lids on both pans (or use tinfoil for the 2-quart one and the lid for the 3-quart), or just put the lid on the 2-quart pan and leave the 3-quart pan uncovered (since the inner pan might stick up too far to fit the 3-quart lid). You can also put coals atop the lid, to spread heat downward.

Build a fire, season permitting, or use a trail stove. If cooking on a stove, medium heat works best. If cooking atop coals, place the pan directly on top of the coals at the edge of the fire (away from the strongest heat). The key is to make sure the pan is not over the coals or stove at such a hot temperature that the bottom and sides burn before the middle has a chance to cook. Cooking time varies according to the heat level, but can be anywhere from 15 to 45 minutes. The muffins are done when you can stick a knife in and the consistency is the same throughout.

Serve warm and enjoy! The final product may not look as pretty as those from a real Dutch oven, but don't tell that to the muffins.

(serves 4)

Variation: Search your surroundings for fresh wild edibles like huckleberries, and add them to the mix.

Black Canyon Chocolate Cake

Molasses works best in this delectable dessert if you don't mind carrying a tiny Nalgene.

> 1½ tablespoons powdered milk
> ¼ cup sweetener (molasses recommended)
> ½ cup chocolate chips
> 1½ tablespoons oil
> ½ cup all-purpose flour
> 1 tablespoon cornstarch
> ¼ teaspoon baking soda
> ⅛ cup powdered sugar

At home: If using a dry sweetener, combine with chocolate chips in a ziplock bag. Also pack flour, cornstarch, and baking soda together. Leave other ingredients separate.

In camp: Mix powdered milk with ¼ cup cold water in a nonstick saucepan. Add sweetener and chocolate chips, and melt over medium heat. Remove from heat and stir in oil, then stir in flour mixture. Pour into a nonstick skillet lined with parchment paper and bake. We recommend the Outback Oven; baking time is about 40 minutes after the thermometer reaches bake. Or you can bake the cake above coals or a fire. Just make sure to rotate the pan periodically, so all parts get heated evenly. (You can also ensure even heating by placing the cake pan inside another pan that's lined with 1-inch-deep pebbles, which distribute heat. Both pans then go atop a fire or stove.) If not using a backcountry oven, it also helps to cover the pan and put coals on top, to apply heat from above. Bake until a fork comes out almost dry. Sprinkle with powdered sugar.

(serves 3)

NO-BAKE TREATS

Peanut Butter Chocolate Bowls

Just like a Reese's Peanut Butter Cup, but way better.

    5 tablespoons butter or margarine
    1/4 cup graham cracker crumbs
    4 ounces (approximately 1 cup) powdered sugar
    1/3 cup chunky peanut butter
    1/3 cup chocolate chips

At home: Mix graham cracker crumbs and sugar, and pack in a ziplock bag. Pack butter, peanut butter, and chocolate chips separately.

In camp: Melt 3 tablespoons of butter and add it to the bag with the crumbs and sugar. Squish bag until it's fully mixed. Add peanut butter and mix again. Scoop mixture into individual bowls. In saucepan, melt 2 tablespoons of butter with the chocolate chips very slowly so chocolate doesn't burn. Pour over peanut butter base. Allow to cool and then dig in.

(serves 2–4, depending on the size of the sweet tooth)

Chocolate Cheesecake

No-bake cheesecake mix makes this dessert easy and fast.

> 2 1.25-ounce packages Mini Oreo Bite Size! Chocolate Sandwich Cookies
> Jell-O No-Bake Real Cheesecake Dessert Mix
> 1/3 cup plus 3 tablespoons powdered milk

At home: Open cheesecake box and pack only the filling mix. Place powdered milk in a ziplock bag.

In camp: To make the crust, crush the cookies inside their bags into a chunky powder. Open bags and pour powder equally into the bottom of four bowls. Mix 1 1/3 cups water (the colder, the better) and powdered milk in a rigid plastic water bottle; shake well. Pour milk into a bowl and add cheesecake mix. Whisk with a fork for 3 minutes or until thick. Spoon over Oreo crust in each of the bowls and enjoy.

(serves 4)

Variations: Use shortbread cookies, Girl Scout Thin Mints, or Golden Oreos for the crust.

For Super Chocolate Cheesecake replace 1/4 cup of the basic cheesecake mix with 1/4 cup instant chocolate pudding mix.

For Lemon Cheesecake replace 1/4 cup of the basic cheesecake mix with 1/4 cup instant lemon pudding mix.

Chef's Secret

Best toppings for cheesecake include these favorites:

Chocolate syrup	M&Ms
Caramel syrup	Crushed Heath bar pieces
Pecans	Dried fruit
Jelly beans	

Chocolate Oatmeal Balls

Or, as Buck Tilton calls them, "Sugary Fat Bombs."
(Remember, fat = good in cold weather.)

1 cup oatmeal (instant or regular)

6 tablespoons butter

6 tablespoons brown sugar

2 or 3 packets hot chocolate mix

1/2 teaspoon vanilla

1 1/2 teaspoons water

In camp: Mix all the ingredients together. Form into little balls with your fingers. Eat immediately, or let them sit until they stiffen (which doesn't take long in the cold).

(serves 3–4)

Camp Tiramisu

Tiramisu sounds complicated and time-consuming, but not if you follow this easy recipe.

1/3 cup water

2 teaspoons instant espresso powder

2 tablespoons Kahlua (get one of those mini-
    bottles from the liquor store)

1 3.4-ounce packet instant white chocolate pudding

2 cups milk (use 2/3 cup powdered milk plus 2 cups
    water)

12–16 ladyfingers

A chunk of good-quality dark chocolate

In camp: Heat water to a boil, then mix in espresso powder and Kahlua. Make pudding according to package directions. Place 6 to 8 ladyfingers in the bottom of a pot; drizzle with half of the espresso mixture, then half of the pudding over it. Repeat to form a second layer. Use a pocketknife to shave thin strips of chocolate on top and serve.

(serves 2–3)

Chewy Fudgy Nutty No-Bake Cookies

For when you need a sugar fix—now.

1 cup brown sugar
$1/4$ cup hot cocoa mix
3 tablespoons powdered milk
5 tablespoons butter
3 tablespoons water
$1^1/3$ cups instant oatmeal
$1/4$ cup chopped walnuts or almonds
$1/2$ teaspoon vanilla

At home: Package sugar, cocoa, and powdered milk in a zip-lock bag. Mix oatmeal and nuts in a separate bag.

In camp: Combine sugar mixture, butter, and water in a pan. Bring to a boil and cook for 3 minutes, stirring constantly. Remove from heat and add the remaining ingredients. Drop spoonfuls onto a plate, pot lid, or another flat surface and cool for 10 minutes.

(Makes about 20 cookies)

Chapter Five

Beverages

Hmm, what do you bring to drink when you go backpacking—a flask of whiskey maybe? Or perhaps you forgo cocktail hour to save weight. But for many there's nothing quite like a sip of something around the campfire at the end of a long day to round out a great trip. Here are a few fun recipes for everything from a warming hot toddy to a fruity frozen cocktail, plus a new twist on everyone's favorite: hot chocolate.

ALCOHOLIC HOT AND COLD DRINKS

Build a Backcountry Bar Kit

Can't decide on just one cocktail for your adventure? Then put together a mobile backcountry bar kit. This kit is geared toward whiskey drinkers, but you can be creative and come up with your own cocktail makings for any liquor type.

The first step in this endeavor is finding a toiletry kit or other closable container in which to store all the necessary ingredients. REI's Stasher Kit is the perfect size, plus it has separate compartments to keep everything organized, zips completely shut, and has a handle on the outside for easy carrying. To properly prepare this mini mobile bar for stocking, you'll also need the following gear (available at www.rei.com):

REI Stasher Kit or similar nylon zip toiletry kit
1 8-ounce flat oval bottle
3 2-ounce flat oval bottles
1 3 x 5-inch ziplock bag

The Ingredients

Once you have all the necessary equipment, the bar will need to be stocked. This will make 5 drinks.

8 ounces whiskey (we like Stranahan's Colorado Whiskey)
$1/2$ ounce vermouth
3 dashes Angostura bitters
$3/4$ ounce simple syrup (equal parts sugar and hot water)
5–8 mint leaves
$3/4$ ounce maple syrup
Small piece of ginger, sliced
1 cinnamon stick
2 cloves
2 slices lemon
1 individual packet of honey
1 packet black tea
1 straw (optional)

At home: Pour 8 ounces whiskey into the 8-ounce bottle. In the three smaller bottles, combine vermouth and bitters in the first; simple syrup and mint in the second; maple syrup, ginger, cinnamon, and cloves in the third. Plan ahead so these ingredients have at least a day to infuse. Lastly, place 2 lemon slices in the small ziplock bag and pack everything into the Stasher Kit.

Hot Toddy

Heat 4 ounces water. Add honey, squeeze of lemon, and 1½ ounces whiskey. Stir to dissolve honey.

Manhattan

Add 1½ ounces whiskey to the smaller bottle (vermouth and bitters). Give a gentle shake to mix, and allow to chill slightly before enjoying (pack in snow or secure in a cold stream).

Upper Peninsula Black Maple Spice

Heat 4 to 6 ounces water and brew black tea per instructions. In a glass, combine tea, 1½ ounces whiskey, squeeze of lemon, and contents of the maple syrup bottle. Stir until dissolved.

Mint Julep

If it's winter or you are up around permanent snow, find a nice clean patch of snow and pack a snowball to fit in your glass. Add 1½ ounces whiskey to the small bottle containing the simple syrup, and shake to mix ingredients. Pour over the top of the snowball and enjoy. Tip: Straw comes in handy here.

Whiskey Neat

Enjoy the remaining 2 ounces of whiskey straight out of the bottle or in a glass with a dash of water.

Pumpkin Spice Toddy

This tempest of flavor is nothing less than fall in a flask. Enjoy in moderation, as alcohol will chill and dehydrate you.

> 2 ounces cream
> 4 tablespoons canned pumpkin pie mix (not pumpkin puree)
> 1/4 ounce unsweetened hazelnut syrup (found in a grocery's coffee section)
> 1 1/2 ounces añejo tequila (we like Milagro Añejo)

In camp: Mix equal parts (by volume) of cream and pumpkin pie mix. Add cream, pie mix, and hazelnut syrup to a pot, and bring to a light boil. Add tequila, stir, and pour into a cup. If desired, garnish with shaved chocolate.

(serves 1)

Wintermint

Leave the Altoids at home. Minty refreshment never tasted so good.

> 1 peppermint tea bag
> 1 1/2 ounces Baileys Irish Cream

In camp: Steep tea for 4 to 7 minutes, add Baileys, enjoy.

(serves 1)

Ginger-Spiced Apple Cider

Warm up with this recipe for apple cider with a kick.

- 3–6 ounces unfiltered apple juice (unfiltered apple cider made from fresh apples is even better)
- 1 individual packet mulling spices
- 1 ounce Domaine de Canton ginger liqueur
- 1 ounce Absolut vanilla vodka
- 1/4 ounce agave nectar

In camp: Heat apple juice with mulling spices and brew according to package directions. Once juice comes to a boil, remove from heat. Add ginger liqueur, vodka, and agave nectar and stir until agave is dissolved.

(serves 1)

Variation: For a Halloween theme in the fall, modify this drink for little ones by leaving out the booze. Miniature Dia de los Muertos–type candy skulls add a fun twist, if you can find them at a Mexican grocery store. They also sweeten the cider as they dissolve. If you can't find candy skulls, check out this idea for a garnish by Martha Stewart: Peel a small apple and carve a face into one side, throw it onto a skewer, and lightly toast over a fire before floating in cider.

South-of-the-Border Coffee

A jolt of caffeine tempered by a shot of tequila.

- 2 cups brewed coffee
- 2 tablespoons powdered milk
- 1 tablespoon brown sugar
- 1 ounce tequila

At home: If you grind your own beans, grind them shortly before you leave home for maximum freshness. Pack the ground beans in a ziplock bag.

In camp: Make the coffee; the rich flavor of a French-pressed cup works well with this recipe. Add the powdered milk, brown sugar, and tequila, stirring gently.

(serves 1)

Variation: Substitute bourbon for tequila for a fine Kentucky coffee.

Icy Alpine Drinks

Cocktails made with snow are a refreshing treat— even in the summer if you are at high-enough altitude!

Mountain Margarita

Lemon-Lime Gatorade + tequila + fresh snow

Watermelon Snowfield

Fruit punch sports drink + Bacardi 51 rum + snow + maraschino cherry

Bikini Sunburn

Vodka + light rum + cherry sours + juice of half a fresh lemon + sugar

Mountain Storm Cosmo

Lime juice + cranberry juice concentrate + triple sec + vodka + lime Kool-Aid powder + hailstones

Snake in the Grass

Lemon-Lime Gatorade + vodka + green crème de menthe

Blackberry Margarita

Fresh-picked berries + snow + tequila

Backcountry Mai Tai

Tang + snow + dark rum

Wilderness White Russian

Kahlua + vodka + milk (use dry whole-milk powder)

Under the Sleeping Bag

Light rum + triple sec + brandy + lemon juice

NONALCOHOLIC HOT DRINKS

The Perfect Après-Ski Drink: Hot Chocolate

Warm up after a day on the slopes with a homemade hot cocoa.

2 cups powdered milk
³/₄ cup sugar
¹/₂ cup unsweetened cocoa
¹/₂ cup mini semisweet chocolate chips
¹/₂ cup powdered nondairy creamer

At home: Place all the ingredients in a bowl and whisk until blended. Pack in a ziplock bag.

In camp / on the slopes: Place 3 or 4 spoonfuls of mix into a mug. Add boiling water, stir, and enjoy.

(serves 12–15)

Variations: Add a dash or two of Baileys Irish Cream, whiskey, rum, peppermint schnapps, or perhaps Jagermeister to liven up your cocoa.

Tangy Hot Apple Cider

Sometimes hot chocolate just doesn't hit the spot.

¹/₄ cup raisins
3 whole cloves
3 cups water
4 packets instant apple cider mix
3 tablespoons Tang
2 cinnamon sticks

At home: Combine the cider mix and Tang in a ziplock bag.

In camp: In a pot, combine raisins, cloves, and water; heat slowly over a low flame until the water is aromatic and amber-colored (about 10 minutes). Remove from heat and stir in the cider mix and Tang. Pour into two large mugs, add a cinnamon stick, and nibble on the raisins (but skip the cloves—they're not very tasty). Or pour the cider through a strainer to remove the chewy bits. This recipe contains lots of vitamin C, which makes this drink a perfect on-the-trail substitute for morning OJ.

(serves 2)

Fruit and Spice Tea

A spicy, refreshing, and warming after-dinner drink.

4 cups water
4½ tablespoons Tang
1 tablespoon instant tea powder
1 tablespoon instant lemonade (presweetened)
About 2 teaspoons cherry Jell-O powder (or experiment with flavors to find your favorite)
¼ teaspoon ground cinnamon
⅛ teaspoon ground cloves
Sugar to taste (optional)

At home: Mix all the dry ingredients in a ziplock bag.

In camp: Boil water. Combine 2 tablespoons (2½ if you prefer stronger tea) of dry mixture and 2 cups hot water. Add a spoonful of sugar if you like. Sip this tea in the morning for a hit of nutrients: Tang is a good source of vitamin A and riboflavin and an excellent source of vitamin C.

(serves 2)

INDEX